CRIMINAL JUSTICE
IN EIGHTEENTH CENTURY MEXICO

CRIMINAL JUSTICE IN EIGHTEENTH CENTURY MEXICO

A Study of the Tribunal of the Acordada

COLIN M. MacLACHLAN

UNIVERSITY OF CALIFORNIA PRESS
Berkeley   Los Angeles   London   1974

University of California Press
Berkeley and Los Angeles, California

University of California Press, Ltd.
London, England

Copyright © 1974 by The Regents of the University of California
ISBN: 0-520-02416-8
Library of Congress Catalog Card Number: 72-97737

CONTENTS

PREFACE ix
  I. INTRODUCTION 1
    Tradition and Philosophy of Spanish Law
      in the Indies
    Conquistadores and the Judiciary in New Spain
  II. EVOLUTION OF THE VICEREGAL JUDICIAL STRUCTURE 21
  III. CRIMINALITY IN THE SOCIAL CONTEXT OF NEW SPAIN 37
  IV. ORGANIZATION AND STRUCTURE 53
  V. ADMINISTRATION OF JUSTICE 69
  VI. ACORDADA AND ITS OPPONENTS 88
  VII. THE LAST DECADE 102
CONCLUSION 108
APPENDIX TABLES 113
NOTES 117
WORKS CITED 132
INDEX 137

PREFACE

How a society seeks to identify and control deviant elements in its midst inevitably reveals its norms. Moreover, law reinforces governmental power and regulates society in a manner consistent with the objectives of the state and the influence of various sectors of the governed. The rule of law can be harsh and narrow or reasonably balanced and widely beneficial, depending on the character and sophistication of the people. Therefore, the study of law, and the institutions created to implement it, is important if one is to understand the functioning of any social system. It is an undeniable fact that practice often differs markedly from the written statutes and to accept the law as written is to confuse an ideal with reality. Nowhere is this more evident than in criminal law where class, social expectations, and race all combine to modify the law as it is applied to different individuals. The reality of the law rests more on the tip of the policeman's baton and the personal prejudices of the local judge than on the written codes. As one moves upward through the judicial system, the gap between theory and practice narrows but never completely disappears.

Relatively little has been written on law enforcement in colonial Mexico or, for that matter, in any other area of Spain's American empire. Charles Gibson makes clear the lack of material on the subject in his useful bibliographical article, *Amerique espagnole coloniale: Introduction bibliographique a l'histoire du droit et a l'ethnologie juridique* (Paris, 1964). My study, which centers on the Tribunal of the Acordada, the most important law enforcement agency in eighteenth-century Mexico, attempts to demonstrate functional law at the enforcement level as well as to indicate the direction or evolution of law in New Spain. The tribunal represented an important stage in the development of the judiciary as well as the state toward the modern ideal of a separation of political and judicial authority. Its creation was a logical outgrowth of the colonial experience. My intent, therefore, is to present the study of law enforcement by the acordada in both its philosophical and institutional contexts.

During the research and writing of this study many demands were made on friends and colleagues. I would like to record my debt to Robert N. Burr and James Lockhart for their dedicated professional assistance. E. Bradford Burns, Richard E. Greenleaf, and Dauril Alden deserve special thanks for their generous advice and encouragement. Jaime E. Rodríguez O., William F. Sater, and James A. Starkweather read parts of the manuscript and offered useful suggestions.

1 INTRODUCTION

Tradition and Philosophy of Spanish Law in the Indies

Hernán Cortés's conquest of the Aztec confederation in 1521 plunged Castile into empire on a scale undreamed of in 1492. Virtually overnight the New World empire burst through its insular limits and washed over the mainland placing a fantastically rich and populous land under the Spanish crown. The swiftness and precision of the conquest of Mexico stunned Spain to the point of disbelief. The very audacity of the conquistadores, the noble deeds and the barbarous cruelty, caused men to wonder at the apparent union of fantasy and reality. The conquest itself appeared to be a romantic triumph over a fabulous empire.[1] On one side stood the haughty conquistador with sword in hand and, on the other, knelt chanting friars at vespers—Spain's mighty alliance of the sword and the cross that ruled a continental empire. While this aspect of the establishment of dominion excited the imagination, it is only part of the story. To be more precise, not only must credit be divided between the conquistador and the friar but also the lawyer (*letrado*), for Spain's legal machinery, at least as powerful as its counterparts in the military and church, consolidated and incorporated the Indian population into the empire.

Law gave permanence as well as form to the initial victories of force and religion. By adjusting the interests of the conquerors and the conquered, Spanish law permitted the organization of empire and assured its survival. Without an acceptable adjustment, Spain could not have turned hordes of Indians into vassals. Castilian law soon became dominant in the New World. Although preconquest Mexico possessed its own laws and customs, they were generally tribal in origin and, consequently, easily overwhelmed by the more sophisticated and complete European codes, backed by the prestige of the conquerors. The absence of a strong native legal tradition made any significant modification of Spanish law in New Spain unnecessary, in spite of Spain's willingness to tolerate, and even enforce, Indian law not in conflict with its interests.[2] It is not surprising, therefore, that law in colonial Mexico remained a transatlantic extension of Spanish law.

In actual operation, law in the Indies did not function in the same manner as in Spain, notwithstanding its basic philosophical purity. The accepted norms of European society which circumscribed individual behavior operated only weakly in the New World. In the absence of a peer society, religious principles and an ingrained respect for social norms, including those legislated into law, were the obvious methods of social control. The individual Spaniard, however, untroubled by the moderating influence of normal social pressure and its restraining force, often acted in a brutal and arbitrary fashion supplying substance to the charges of inhuman treatment of the Indians leveled by more disciplined individuals such as Bartolomé de las Casas. Father Las Casas, unlike the rough conquistadores, could rely on his deeply held religious beliefs to restrain lapses in the accepted norms of Spanish society. The New World was a frontier situation and its aboriginal inhabitants, unprotected by an understanding of European social structures, could be exploited at the whim of the conquerors. Such behavior, which would not have been tolerated in Spain, undoubtedly posed a problem but it did not require a philosophical modification of law. It was a technical problem that could be dealt with through the normal legislative process. Obviously, the Indian needed protection in the face of the uncontrolled demands of Spanish settlers. This was a matter of judicial balance, however, and could be achieved within the existing framework of Spanish law. By making the Indian a legal minor entitled to special protection, the crown theoretically brought the disproportionate power of the Spanish population into balance.[3]

The first major piece of legislation formulated especially for the New World was the Laws of Burgos of 1512 which attempted to regulate European-Indian relations. After Cortés's successful seizure of the Aztec confederation, additional supplementary laws soon would be issued in an ever-increasing flood. Because the crown held its American empire by proprietary right, the kings' ministers were encouraged to enact legislation freely, much of it very narrow and formulated without adequate attention to the general context of the law in the Indies.[4] Laws designed solely for the Spanish Indies, although gathered together and published as a separate code in 1680 and again in 1791, never lost their supplementary character. Only in administrative law, or what might be termed constitutional law, did these codes even approach being definitive. In civil and criminal matters the laws of the Indies made no pretense of completeness. Significantly, the *Recopilación de leyes de los Reynos de las Indias* of 1791 does not include any legislation after the reign of Charles II (1665–1700). Philip V, first of the Spanish Bourbons, and his successors continued to direct special instructions to the colonies, but such legislation was not considered part of a distinct and separate code. As before, laws issued in Spain automatically applied in the Indies unless specifically excluded. The *Recopilación* of 1791 fixed the order of application of Spanish law, when an issue could not be settled by the supplementary laws of the Indies, as follows: the laws of Castile as collected in the *Nueva recopilación de Castilla* (1569) followed by the Laws of Toro (1505), which also included a further ranking of pertinent codes. An attempt to formulate a special code applicable only to the Indies failed. Charles IV, who approved the first book of the *Nuevo código de leyes de Indias* in 1792, ordered, however, that each individual law required a royal decree before it could be considered in effect. The antagonism of the Council of the Indies and the king's indecision combined to doom the project.[5] Consequently, colonial judicial officials continued to refer to the laws of Spain in order to impose penalties. Technically, a judge could go from the laws of the Indies through six separate Spanish codes to settle a case.[6] A Spanish official formally sentencing an Indian delinquent in New Spain not only physically represented the Iberian legal heritage but the sentence itself had in many instances been set prior to the discovery of America. The roots of colonial law remained firmly embedded in Spanish soil. Thus, in order to understand the operation and philosophy of law in New Spain, its European origins must be traced.

Law in the Iberian peninsula developed in a series of cultural overlays that made it incredibly rich and diverse and at the same time complicated its study. A distinctly Iberian legal tradition began to emerge with the imposition of Roman rule. Interested above all else in incorporating people and their wealth into the empire, Rome willingly permitted the conquered people to retain their laws and legal customs except when such laws seriously conflicted with Roman interests. As a consequence, civil and commercial law that touched on the commercial unity and prosperity of Rome and its empire received the heavy imprint of imperial legislation, while laws that dealt with adjusting the conflicts arising among members of a particular society remained intact and functioning alongside the laws of Rome. Toleration of a *jus gentium* with its roots firmly implanted in pre-Roman Spain permitted Rome to rule without restructuring and reorganizing the many individual societies incorporated into the empire. The pragmatic nature of Roman rule contributed to its success. Such flexibility continued to be the principal feature of law even after the *Constitutio Antoniniana* (A.D. 212) extended Roman citizenship to nearly all the free ininhabitants of the empire. In theory citizenship brought with it the benefits and responsibilities of Roman law, removing the new citizen from the jurisdiction of their cities (*civitates*). In actual fact, imperial law did not displace the old laws and customs. Rome, by this time a declining power, could hardly impose the acceptance of its laws as a condition of citizenship even if it so desired. The main thrust behind the extension of citizenship was the hope that such a measure would restore strength and unity to the crumbling foundations of the Roman Empire. The actual acceptance of Roman law became a secondary matter. In addition, the lack of trained jurisconsults among the new Romans made displacement of the old codes technically difficult if not impossible. More than likely the only effect of the Constitutio Antoniniana was the corruption of both Roman law and local legal customs in Iberia.[7]

To the laws of the Hispano-Romans the Visigoths added a new element. Entering the Iberian peninsula in the middle of the fifth century, first as Roman mercenaries and later as de facto rulers, they brought their own germanic laws. Outnumbered, perhaps as much as ten to one, the Visigoths made no attempt to impose their codes on the subjugated population.[8] Moreover, long impressed by the grandeur of Rome, they had no intention of eradicating those aspects of Roman culture not in conflict with their sovereignty. The new rulers, in exchange for order among the conquered population, supported what amounted to a Hispano-Roman jus gentium in Iberia. The Visigothic King Alaric II, in the year 506, even codified and arranged Roman law in his *Lex Romana Visigothorum*. The close contact between the Visigoths and their Hispano-Roman subjects, however, eroded legal differences. In 546 King Theudes (531–548) enacted legislation, concerning civil litigation expenses which applied to all inhabitants.[9] The double system of separate codes and legal customs received a damaging blow when King Reccared abandoned the Arian heresy and embraced orthodox Christianity (587). With the collapse of religious barriers, the fusion of the two elements became inevitable as well as desirable. By the seventh century evidence of the amalgamation of the Visigoths and the Hispano-Romans appeared in legal form with the issuance of a code that combined Roman and Visigothic law—the *Fuero Juzgo*. Although far from being accepted as the standard code, it served as the principal uniform legal code down to 1254 or 1255, when a more ambitious codification incorporated and superseded it.[10]

Two other invasions of the Iberian peninsula also left their mark, although just how much impact they had on law is uncertain. The expansion of the Eastern empire under Justinian established a Byzantine foothold in Iberia. The Byzantines, however, failed to topple the Visigoths and they only lasted from 554 to the reign of Swinthila (621–631).[11] Their effect on law could only have been minimal. The Moorish conquest and occupation of Spain from 711 to the collapse of its last stronghold in Granada in 1492 obviously was of greater consequence and deeply influenced Spanish life and society. Yet, the Moorish impact on law did not equal its influence on medicine, architecture, and administration. Like the Romans and the early Visigoths, the Muslim rulers of Spain tolerated a jus gentium permitting the subject population to retain its laws and legal traditions.[12] As before, only those customs and laws that conflicted with the interests of the conquerors faced modification. As a result the Moors modified laws dealing with property and agricultural privileges, such as water rights, while laws dealing with the intrasocietal relations of the subject people remained relatively untouched.

While direct Muslim influence on the legal traditions of Spain did not radically modify previous customs, the disruptive effect of the conquest itself destroyed much of the efforts of the Visigoths, after the conversion of Reccared, to unite the population under one legal system. The Fuero Juzgo aimed at social and political unification in the midst of the Moorish conquest. Perhaps the attempted legal unification could not have been made at a more difficult time. The hard-pressed Christians had been driven back into the Cantabrian Mountains. There they were fragmented into tiny states, and the ideal of political and social unity through the laws gave way to a more pressing concern for survival. As the situation stabilized and the Christian states began the long and protracted offensive toward reconquest, the ideal of universal law fell before the realities of the feudal system. Weak Christian monarchies made political alliances with powerful interests in an effort to maintain their theoretically supreme position. At the same time, such desperate maneuvers, in the face of demands of powerful nobles, cities, and even monasteries that had become virtually sovereign, created a political crisis for the fragile monarchies. By presiding over the dissipation and dispersal of their powers they avoided an outright collapse of the institution of monarchy but in the process found themselves unable to demonstrate the advantages of retaining a central source of power. The monarchy, unable to effectively arbitrate and coordinate the many and often conflicting interests of society, came very close to sinking into the social morass of feudalism.[13]

Alfonso X, the Wise (*el sabio*), who claimed the throne of Castile and León in 1252, wrestled with the problem, arriving at a compromise that reaffirmed the principle of legal unity under the laws of the crown, while conceding the impossibility of requiring universal acceptance or substitution of regional customs and privileges by a royal code. The *Fuero Real* (1255) of Alfonso attempted to codify all existing fueros placing them within a "crown" fuero. By throwing the royal mantle over local laws and customs, the king sought to reestablish the position of the crown as the supreme judicial and legislative source in the realm. He in effect granted privileges that already existed based on regional fueros. The effort of the crown to coopt local and regional judicial customs reestablished royal judicial and legislative prerogatives but little else. The not unexpected operational failure of the Fuero Real stemmed from the weakness of the crown in relation to powerful conflicting interests that firmly resisted any expansion of royal powers. Regional fueros continued to enjoy a stricter allegiance than any universal code, be it Roman, Visigothic, or their combination in the Fuero Juzgo and the Fuero Real.[14]

Regional fueros, however, were not the only barriers faced by a resurgent monarchy. To compound the legal maze, each class also had its own particular fuero. Much of the strength of class privileges sprang from the lack of codification, permitting endless bickering over tradition and, through judicious interpretation, an extension of privileges. Adherence to class as well as regional fueros provided an important element of social cohesion. This complex problem, which had its roots entwined around the very essence of society, made the struggle of the crown to gain control of law, and hence political power, in reality a struggle to restructure society in Castile.

The efforts of the monarchy to impose its will through a universal legal code received technical as well as philosophical assistance from the revival of Roman law in the eleventh century. Scholarly examination of Roman law, principally Justinian's *Corpus Juris Civilis*, was used to lay the foundation of legal science. At Bologna, one of the major centers for the study of Roman law, students from all parts of Europe, including Spain, sought universal legal principles. Known as the glossators, because of their methods of making marginal notations (glosses), they confined themselves to Roman law, ignoring existing legal codes. The next logical step, that of examining functioning codes, was undertaken by a new school of thought, the postglossators or commentators of the thirteenth and fourteenth centuries. Their learned "commentaries" combined the principles of Roman law with canon law and municipal codes, through which they attempted to find a universal strand. Their pragmatic search for legal universalism influenced the development of crown law in Spain.

The clearest indication of such influence appears in the *Siete Partidas* (1265) of Alfonso X. Although infused with Germanic and feudal principles, major sections taken from the Corpus Juris Civilis made it much more than a feudal code.[15] Never promulgated during the lifetime of Alfonso the Wise, it nevertheless had a major influence on Castilian legal philosophy. The Partidas reinforced the tendency of jurists, already steeped in the study of

Roman law, to supplement regional fueros with universal principles derived from Justinian's code. Roman law thus served as a weak but definite unifying strand running through the confused and fragmented mass of Castilian law. The Siete Partidas eventually received official sanction within the *Ordenamiento de Alcalá de Henares* (1348). The Ordenamiento set the order of application of the law as (1) the Ordenamiento; (2) the municipal fueros; (3) the Fuero Real; and, finally, (4) the Siete Partidas.[16] It is interesting to note that the prescribed order subordinated the Partidas to codes that it had attempted to absorb. The Ordenamiento would remain the dominant royal code until the major revisions implemented by the Catholic kings in the early sixteenth century.

The issuance of royal codes remained a literary exercise as long as the crown lacked the power to suppress or modify territorial fueros to meet the needs of a centralized monarchy. The establishment of a judicial principle, however important in itself, did not give the crown the force necessary to impose its will on powerful interest groups. In order to give some substance to its decrees, the monarchy required enforcement powers as well as the general acceptance of its right to legislate superior codes. Without enforcement, political control rested on the vague and often undependable foundations of tradition and custom. The attempt to establish effective judicial institutions capable of imposing the king's law was in effect an effort to concentrate political power under the centralized monarchy. Law and its enforcement eventually became the cutting edge of royal power and would be so regarded by the Castilian monarchs.

The formation of powerful judicial organizations could only be accomplished over a considerable period of time. Until the middle of the thirteenth century justice remained more personal than institutional. When the king dispensed justice he surrounded himself with favored magnates meeting as the *curia* or *cort*. The members of this informal tribunal constantly changed and its decisions depended on the momentary whim of the monarch and his temporary advisors who were guided only by the vague outlines of tradition. While individually important, such decisions added little to the growth of an institutionalized body of law. In addition, the sovereign often utilized his council to serve in place of the curia. The royal administration of justice clearly lacked an institutional framework to assure its continuity.[17]

It was not surprising that Alfonso X, who fully appreciated the connection between law and political power, made the first attempt to institutionalize Castilian law. In 1274, under the Ordinance of the Cortes de Zamora, King Alfonso formed a royal tribunal composed of twenty-three *alcaldes de corte*. A higher court of three judges, familiar with regional and class fueros, was to receive appeals. The Ordinance specified those crimes that fell to the royal cognizance and those that could be appealed to the higher court. Originally the king intended to devote three days a week to the administration of justice. The press of state affairs, however, quickly reduced the monarch's attendance to one day. In the absence of the king, the tribunal met under an *adelantado del rey* or *sobrejuez*. Unfortunately, these judicial institutions declined with the death of their originator but they nevertheless represented an important step in institutionalizing the power of the monarchy.[18]

During the reign of King Henry II (1369–1379) the royal tribunal would be revived as the *audiencia*. In 1387 the royal audiencia extended its influence outside the immediate court by dividing its sessions between Medina del Campo, Olmedo, Alcalá de Henares, and Madrid. Shortly thereafter an audiencia was established at Segovia (1390) and at Valladolid (1405). Because these courts were separated from the presence of the monarch, they often lost their effectiveness when faced with the pressure of a powerful aristocracy. In 1433 a major reorganization divided the audiencias into two principal sections (*salas*), one for civil and the other for criminal cases. A lesser sala to hear cases involving the aristocracy attempted to interpose the crown as the mediator between the classes.[19] The actual power of the audiencias was hardly impressive but their existence, even if ineffectual, represented a positive step toward the concentration of power under the monarchy.

The king's justice, as exercised by the audiencias, seldom directly touched the everyday life of the common man. Local fueros, confirmed by the crown, placed the administration of justice in the hands of municipal alcaldes selected by the city councils themselves. In an effort to influence local justice, the crown dispatched representatives (*pesquisidores*) to the municipalities to investigate adminstration of the fueros. Firmer royal control at the lower levels came with the imposition of *corregidores* during the reign of

Alfonso XI (1312–1350).²⁰ These officials, armed with the full prestige of the monarchy, were given judicial functions and a place on the municipal councils. In spite of resistance, the corregidores brought the cities under the direct political influence of the crown.

When Isabella proclaimed herself queen of Castile in 1474, the monarchy had already forged the tools necessary to impose royal control. It only remained for the crown to add strong leadership and a sense of political strategy—qualities the new queen possessed and willingly utilized. Law and its enforcement in the hands of the queen became a sword with which she attempted to reduce those interests in conflict with the powers of the monarchy. Isabella chose the *hermandades* as one of her primary weapons.

The hermandades, whose roots have been traced as far back as the year 1110, originated in the general insecurity of life and property which plagued the Iberian peninsula during the reconquest.²¹ Organized by municipal authorities as brotherhoods of local volunteers to maintain law and order on the roads surrounding their towns, the hermandades rendered invaluable service to their municipalities. Reliance on their own resources to maintain order inevitably strengthened the town's political power, enabling them to resist the incursions of local magnates. In 1465 the hermandades formed a confederation, drawing up a set of laws and ordinances that provided for a standard organization of the brotherhoods in each locality. A *junta general* made up of delegates from the different provincial brotherhoods exercised central control. The consolidation of municipal power under a central junta obviously posed a threat to the crown's desire to centralize power in its own hands. Isabella not only ended this danger but turned the hermandades into a coercive instrument of royal power. Under the direction of the queen, the brotherhoods played a significant role in the successful consolidation of the monarchy under the Catholic kings.

Skillfully taking advantage of the political turmoil of the times, Isabella obtained general agreement for a reorganization of the hermandades under crown control.²² Based on the monarch's proclamation at the Cortes of Madrigal (1476), municipal representatives drew up a constitution to govern the expanded brotherhood. The reorganization provided for a supreme council of the hermandad presided over by the bishop of Cartagena acting as the queen's representative. Armed with the prestige of the crown and a kingdom-wide organization, the santa hermandad, as it was now called, effectively wielded its police powers. The Holy Brotherhood received complete jurisdiction over certain classes of crimes with full authority to punish those apprehended. Royal ordinances prevented the unnecessary interference of local judicial authorities in hermandad cases. The queen even attempted to force all classes, including the nobility, to contribute to the support of the brotherhood, regardless of ancient privileges that exempted certain groups from taxation. In the face of complaints, however, the crown agreed to respect traditional exemptions.[23]

Queen Isabella employed the hermandad to protect and reclaim royal prerogatives. While the armed power of the brotherhood hardly matched that of the powerful aristocracy, it was sufficient to back up her insistence that crown authority be respected. The right of the monarchy to impose its authority over the personal justice exercised by the nobility would be strengthened in 1476 when alcaldes of the hermandad received permission to enter private estates to search for criminals. The following year private imprisonment for debt was ordered abolished and in 1485 all private confinement became illegal. Although the crown won acceptance of such powers on paper, it is unlikely these orders could be enforced. Nevertheless, the issuance of these decrees established important precedents. In 1480 the Act of Resumption, another symbolic victory attained by an increasingly confident monarch, transferred revenue totaling thirty million maravedis from the nobility to the crown. Although little was actually returned, it served to emphasize the crown's determination to assert its primacy over the aristocracy.[24]

Isabella's use of the hermandad to reinforce her authority throughout the kingdom and the taxes imposed for support of the organization resulted in increasing pressure upon her to abolish the institution. In 1498 a politically secure monarchy gracefully bowed to pressure and abolished the junta general of the Holy Brotherhood as well as all salaried positions.[25] The hermandades continued to exist as local rural police organizations but ceased to be utilized by the crown for political purposes.

In conjunction with the political deployment of the santa hermanded, Isabella took steps to make the crown's judicial institutions function more effectively. As a preliminary move, the Council of Castile received instruction to devote more consideration to judicial matters. In 1480 the location of the audiencia was permanently fixed at Valladolid, and in 1494 another royal court was established at Ciudad Real; this audiencia would be moved to Granada in 1505. The audiencias of Valladolid and Granada recevied the higher status of *chancillerías* and subsequently became appellate courts, hearing appeals from lesser audiencias.[26] At the local level the crown expanded the power of the corregidores, and by 1480 all Castilian cities functioned under the watchful eyes of these royal officials.[27] Under the Catholic kings, the crown's ability to adjudicate conflicting interests without resorting to warfare was firmly established.

While the judicial structure became more effective, efforts to modify or absorb conflicting fueros within royal codes continued. Here Isabella met with only limited success; nevertheless, some gains would be made. Jurist Díaz de Montalvo, acting under a crown commission, collected ordinances and pragmatics not included in existing codes and published the collection as the *Ordenanzas Reales* in 1484.[28] Mere compilations, while useful, did not solve the legal and political problem of competing regional fueros. A more ambitious attempt, aimed at absorbing competing codes, would be made at the Cortes of Toledo (1505). A series of separate enactments known as the *Leyes de Toro* imposed, among other things, an order of application of all previous codes. Subsequently, the order sanctioned by the acts of Toro would be incorporated into the *Nueva recopilación de Castilla* (1567) and remained valid into the nineteenth century, being reaffirmed in the *Novísima recopilación de las leyes de España* in 1805.[29]

In the midst of the struggle for royal supremacy, Christopher Columbus returned from his initial voyage of discovery with news of exotic lands that he had placed under the crown of Castile. The discoverer also laid claim to the generous privileges conceded by the queen in the *Capitulación* of Santa Fe, which appointed Columbus and his heirs virtual lords of the lands that he discovered. Ironically, Columbus pressed his claims just as the Catholic kings had succeeded in reducing the independent power of the nobility. It soon became evident that the Admiral of the Ocean Seas had established Spanish claims to a series of islands populated by barbarous Indians, certainly exotic, but hardly threatening to the political position of the monarchy. In spite of this, Columbus quickly found his powers under attack and, under various pretexts, his many privileges reverting to the crown. Almost instinctively the monarchy moved to absorb his prerogatives just as it had done with those of powerful interest groups in Spain itself. As in Castile, the judiciary brought the coercive might of the kingdom to bear on the claims of the discoverer. The establishment of the audiencia of Santo Domingo in 1511 virtually assured the nullification of the privileges rashly granted Columbus prior to his success.[30] The heirs of the discoverer turned to the courts in a pathetic attempt at redress only to sink into a veritable mire of legal procedures and appeals.

With Cortés's conquest of Mexico, the crown faced a much more difficult challenge to its political supremacy. The very magnitude of the Western Hemisphere not only staggered the mind but obviously outstripped the financial and planning resources of the monarchy. Consequently, Spain permitted the private conquest of its empire, undertaken at little actual expense to the crown, in return for vague and often illusory privileges for the conqueror. While such concessions succeeded in motivating individual initiative they posed a potential threat to royal control. As in the past, the monarchy again turned to the judiciary as its prime defensive weapon. Cortés, at the very height of his power and glory, found his power countered by a newly dispatched audiencia. Although the audiencia quickly abused its authority and had to be reorganized, it successfully achieved its principal objective—that of stripping Cortés of political control.[31] While he would be mollified somewhat by a large land grant and the title of Marqués del Valle de Oaxaca, he fully realized that actual political power had been wrenched from his hands. The political success achieved by the audiencia of Mexico led to the establishment of other audiencias throughout the empire. Even after the introduction of the viceregal system, the judiciary continued to be primarily a political instrument clothed in judicial robes.

That the judiciary should assume a political role in the New World was hardly surprising. The use of law and the administration of justice had played an important part in the establishment of a centralized monarchy in Castile. The political supremacy of the crown emerged simultaneously with the discovery of America, and with hardly a broken step the monarchy would use the judiciary in the New World as it had done so successfully in the Old. Hernán Cortés rightly feared the crown's lawyers. Out of Spain's legal tradition arose a philosophy that colored the functioning of the legal system in New Spain as well as in other parts of the empire. Spanish law developed an amorphous quality that flowed over regional laws and customs engulfing rather than suppressing. The crown seldom suppressed undesirable or outmoded institutions, preferring instead to merge titles and jurisdictions into a new organization. Such cautious tactics avoided a violent reaction to the extension of royal power, enabling the crown to build its strength on precedent. Consequently the monarchy developed a fine appreciation of the political utility of law, with a corresponding lack of concern for the public benefits stemming from a just and efficient administration of the law. The social benefits were viewed as tangential, albeit desirable, by-products of the judicial system. The crown's struggle to establish its authority, in the face of *conquistadores* determined to enjoy the political and material benefits of their herculean efforts, reinforced its tendency to employ the judiciary for political purposes. Unfortunately, throughout the colonial period, Spanish legal philosophy never quite shed its essentially feudal concerns.

Conquistadores and the Judiciary in New Spain

When Hernán Cortés and his men seized control of the valley of Mexico, the political seat of the Mexican confederation, they assumed the command of a well-ordered Indian society that had already learned the value of social cooperation. The indigenous inhabitants lived under laws and within a political structure in some aspects superior to their European contemporaries. A simple, but effective, sociopolitical organization permitted the conquerors to govern through the established channels of authority. Cortés's political caution, coupled with the natural desire of the Indians to continue their orderly existence, made it possible for the Spaniards to hold the vast territory for the Castilian monarchy. The crown, represented by a small band of soldiers of fortune, assumed sovereignty over an Indian population estimated to be in the millions; this was an extraordinary feat made possible only by preserving the political structure of a people sufficiently civilized to order themselves.[32]

The Europeans, observing the functioning of Indian society, applied Spanish political theory to explain its operation. Key Indian officials were soon singled out and given Spanish titles that seemed the most appropriate to their actual functions. Thus, the tribal parentela unit, the *calpulli*, which elected its own council and governed a particular district, was equated with the Spanish *barrio*, and its council with the standard Spanish municipal council, the *ayuntamiento*. The various elders and chiefs—who did not hold their office by right of inheritance—were mistaken by the conquerors for a hereditary nobility.[33] While the feudal concept of a natural lord (*señor natural*) was hardly accurate, it fitted the Indian authorities into an acceptable European framework and at the same time implied the obligation of the "Indian nobility" to support their feudal suzerains.[34] The Spaniards applied the Arawak term *cacique* to the members of the newly hereditary nobility. As caciques and part of the *hidalguía* of the Kingdom of New Spain, Indian nobles were entitled to be addressed with the respectful title of don. The distortion of lines of authority must have been somewhat confusing to the indigenous population, but such changes could be accepted without much difficulty. The absorption of Indian officials within a Spanish political framework would eventually lead to their loss of effective political power. Meanwhile, Indian authorities operating under Spanish supervision helped maintain order in the colony for at least the crucial first half-century of Spanish rule.

The relatively smooth internal operation of the subjugated Indian societies freed the conquerors and the crown to devote their energy to the struggle for political supremacy in New Spain. The contest between the conquistadores and their king involved the traditional issue of centralization of power aligned against fragmentary and competing sources of power. Very simply, the transplanted Europeans viewed their participation in the conquest as entitling them to the political and economic rewards of empire. The internecine battle surged around the introduction of the *en-*

comienda system. First introduced into the Antilles, the encomienda provided for the division of tributory Indians among deserving Spaniards. The *encomendero*, in return for tribute in labor or kind, provided the Indians with guidance and protection, but, more important, the state in turn was provided help with certain administrative responsibilities and a source for military service. It was a convenient way of rewarding the efforts of the conqueror while preserving military power in case of an Indian insurrection. Although the institution had historical roots in Spain itself, its feudal overtones displeased the monarchy. The crown did not desire to preside over potentially threatening feudal fiefdoms. Moreover, the encomienda system had worked to the detriment of the island Indians, persuading the crown that it should be suppressed. The decision against the encomienda had been made even before the conquest of Mexico.[35]

Ironically, Cortés himself originally opposed the institution based on his observation in the Antilles; however, once faced with the problem of organizing the conquest, providing for military security, and rewarding companions in arms, he revised his views. Cortés seized upon the encomienda as the most expedient method available. Well aware of the controversy over the system, he defended his actions to Emperor Charles V on the basis that circumstances left him no alternative. Almost as an afterthought the conqueror attempted to cover up his ruthless pragmatism by noting that the Indians of New Spain would not react as adversely as those in the Antilles, especially in view of some minor change he had instituted. Such excuses did not please the crown, which replied by ordering Cortés to revoke any grants already made and refrain from creating new ones. Undaunted, Cortés ignored the emperor's instructions and advised the court that to suppress the encomienda would jeopardize Spanish sovereignty. To make his views absolutely clear, he posed a rhetorical question: Who would hold the country for the emperor if the conquerors were denied their reward? Confidently, even arrogantly, Cortés had presented the crown with an unacceptable alternative to the encomienda system—either accept it or hold the territory without the aid of the conquistadores.[36] Emperor Charles V, well aware of his dependence on private initiative—given the chronically depleted treasury—could only have been humiliated by the brutal treatment accorded his sensibilities by the self-confident Cortés.

The conqueror's less than moral victory, however displeasing to the crown, forced the monarchy to face reality. Unless the power of such men as Cortés was contained, Spain risked the formation of a semifeudal kingdom in New Spain. A colony based on a quasi-feudal institution that elevated Spanish noblemen over tributary Indian subjects would make the centralized power of the monarchy illusory. Almost instinctively, the monarchy searched for a judicial weapon to parry the political thrust of the encomenderos. In 1526 Charles V dispatched a judge (*juez de residencia*) to investigate Cortés's conduct as governor of the new kingdom. The inopportune death of the official, however, left the powers of the conqueror uncontested. An increasingly concerned crown now appointed an audiencia (1528) whose president, Beltrán Nuño de Guzmán, was an archenemy of Cortés. Clothed in the judicial robes of an *oidor*, the ruthless Guzmán despoiled Cortés and his partisans of much of their economic and political power.[37] These excesses led to the reconstitution of the audiencia in 1530. The members of the reformed institution, all respected lawyers, received secret instructions to consolidate royal authority and continue to exclude the conqueror and his followers from political authority, while at the same time cutting down the power of the Guzmán faction. Those encomiendas distributed by the first audiencia were to be incorporated under the crown. Significantly, the restoration of encomiendas stripped from the Cortés faction by Guzmán was not seriously considered. The monarch ordered the placing of crown encomiendas under a royal official—the corregidor. The establishment of *corregimientos* in New Spain represented the crown's response to Cortés's arrogant challenge to work out an alternative to the encomienda system.

The corregimiento aimed at the eventual absorption of the encomienda within the royal system of government. A deposed encomendero, if considered worthy, could be compensated by being appointed a corregidor: in effect being transformed from a semi-feudal lord to a royal official in a move worthy of the political genius of Alfonso the Wise. The second audiencia did not end the competing political and economic power of the conquistadores. It did, however, establish an uneasy balance of power in the crown's favor.

The next step in the consolidation of royal authority came in 1535 with the introduction of the viceregal system and the arrival of the first viceroy, Antonio de Mendoza. Vested with the supplementary titles of governor, captain-general, and president of the audiencia, Viceroy Mendoza became the direct representative of the monarch. His appointment could be relied on to awe the socially pretentious encomenderos—he was selected from among the most distinguished families of Spain. Significantly, the following year, the crown with its continuing dependence on the military potential of the conquistadores and their sons was forced to legalize the inheritance of encomiendas by the son or widow of the grantee, thus extending the possession of the grant for two lives. This did not satisfy the pressure to make possession perpetual but, nonetheless, represented a concession to the encomendero class.[38]

The military insecurity of the crown and its caution not to alienate the encomenderos was justified by events. With the outbreak of the Mixton war in 1541, Spain faced a major challenge to its sovereignty. Rebellious Indians provoked into violence by the abuses heaped on them by Europeans actually endangered the city of Guadalajara. But perhaps even more serious than the threatened loss of an important regional center was the possibility of the revolt spreading throughout New Spain, as the abused Indian population seized the opportunity to avenge itself. An old conquistador, Pedro de Alvarado, attempted to duplicate the daring of the earlier days of the conquest only to find that a small and fearless band of Spaniards no longer could overwhelm Indian warriors. Viceroy Mendoza, greatly alarmed, took to the field himself. Taking a calculated risk, he armed and mounted Indian allies to assist the Spaniards in containing the insurrection.[39] The arming of the always suspect Indian testified both to the fear of the Europeans and the seriousness of the situation. Mendoza's successful campaign as well as the use of the loyal Indian allies bolstered the prestige of the viceregal government, signaling the end of the crown's psychological dependence on the encomenderos.[40]

The growing confidence of the crown in its ability to hold New Spain without relying on the might of the former conquistadors or their heirs took on the form of the devastating New Laws of 1542. Many of the privileges the encomenderos had considered well established were abolished by the New Laws, but of most concern

Introduction 19

was article thirty-five which prohibited the distribution of new encomiendas and required that established ones be reincorporated into the crown on the death of the incumbent. Such action proved premature; fortunately Viceroy Mendoza joined with the outraged encomenderos to convince the royal official sent to implement the laws to suspend them pending an appeal.[41] Had the viceroy failed to act so prudently, civil war might have resulted. Pressure forced a reversal of article thirty-five but the other restrictions remained valid. Further legal action in 1549 eliminated labor tribute, confining the holder of an encomienda to a set tribute in kind or money.[42] The encomienda thus took on the aspects of a royal pension stripped of political power and dependent on the indulgence of the crown.

The limitations placed on the encomienda left a resentful group, bitter and economically insecure, concerned that the crown would eventually divest them of what they considered their birthright. Their deep frustration eventually led to treason and a conspiracy to create a semifeudal kingdom independent of the crown of Castile. Thus, the conspirators gathered around Martín Cortés, the conqueror's son and heir, who arrived in Mexico in 1563. The second Marqués del Valle de Oaxaca became the symbolic hero of the frustrated sons of the conquistadores. In addition the Indians transferred to his son their personal loyalty to Cortés. Unfortunately, the inherited mantle of Hernán Cortés did not transform an immature and overly pretentious Spanish aristocrat into a responsible leader. The potential for treason was heightened by internal squabbles within the viceregal government which resulted in an open split between the viceroy (Velasco) and the audiencia. The subsequent death of the viceroy, leaving power in the hands of the audiencia, deprived New Spain of its administrative and political head. To add to the confusion, a royal *visitador* sent to investigate the causes of the quarrel did little except aggravate factionalism. In the midst of the political tension, treason flourished.

The conspiracy, guided by Alonso and Gil González de Avila, the heirs of a conquistador and encomendero, called for a quick coup d'etat followed by the proclamation of Cortés as king to be legitimatized by a parliament of assembled notables. The marquis himself wavered but the González brothers felt confident he could be dragged along by events. At the last minute, the sickness of one of the conspirators disrupted the plans. Meanwhile, the audiencia, aware of the plot but unsure of their powers, remained paralyzed until Cortés's indecision became evident. The judges, then lured the marquis into their chambers placing him under arrest. Subsequently, the two major conspirators were arrested, tried for high treason, and beheaded on October 3, 1566, causing panic among those who had been associated with the scheme. The arrival of a new viceroy, who insisted that Cortés be returned to Spain for trial and whose attitude alienated the audiencia, did little to calm the situation.[43]

Philip II, who received only the audiencia's version of the conspiracy as well as its allegation that the new viceroy sympathized with the rebels, responded by dispatching Alonso de Muñoz. Armed with extreme powers to ferret out treason, Muñoz engaged in a reign of terror arresting and executing those suspected of complicity. When news of the judge's excesses reached Spain, Philip ordered his immediate removal. Muñoz's cruel zeal, while condemned by the king, succeeded, however, in pulling feudal political ambitions out by the roots.[44] The struggle over the encomienda system and the subsequent conspiracy confirmed the crown's fears. The political insecurity of the Castilian monarchy, which had shaped Spanish judicial institutions in the Old World, would continue to do so in the New.

2 EVOLUTION OF THE VICEREGAL JUDICIAL STRUCTURE

In New Spain the needs of justice were served by political institutions that exercised various judicial functions as an adjunct to their political authority. The subordination of justice within political institutions was a natural result of the philosophical development of the monarchy. Jurisdiction constituted the essence of the medieval concept of sovereignty accepted by the Castilian crown. Such a concept drew no real distinction between judicial and political objectives. The monarch's position as supreme arbritrator between the classes depended on the acceptance of the king's right to impose his will. In effect the crown's political power rested on its ability to enforce royal jurisdiction. Consequently, political and judicial functions were fused, not only in the collective mind of Castile but in its institutions. Thus, the viceroy of the kingdom of New Spain became the chief magistrate of the realm, although his political functions were more important than his judicial responsibilities.[1] In addition, the physical distance separating the king of Spain from his empire tended to emphasize the political duties of the viceroy as well as other royal officials charged with both political and judicial functions.[2] All crown officials, including the viceroy, combined judicial functions with political and administrative responsibilities that in reality were of paramount importance.

The audiencia, the highest court in the viceroyalty, provides a clear example of the fusion of justice and political admininstration. Divided into two salas, civil and criminal (*sala del crimen*), the audiencia possessed appellate authority over all cases decided upon by crown or municipal magistrates. In addition to accepting appeals, the court approved, before execution, all major sentences of judicial officials, thus technically reviewing the actions of inferior magistrates throughout the viceroyalty.[3] In the immediate area of its residence and for a radius of five leagues around the capital, the audiencia, through the sala del crimen, legally exercised justice in the first instance. In actuality the sala del crimen of the audiencia of Mexico also appointed agents outside the five league area. This practice, originally necessitated by the abnormal circumstances of the conquest, continued until 1767. In that year the crown, pressured by the viceroy, the Marqués de Croix who expressed little faith in the abilities of the sala, ordered the audiencia to respect the area limitations prescribed by law.[4] As a primary tribunal within the prescribed area, the audiencia directly engaged in law enforcement. Agents of the criminal chamber patrolled the streets apprehending delinquents and bringing them before the *alcaldes del crimen* of the court. Certain crimes, occurring within the viceroyalty, which fell into the category of *casos de corte*, such as murder, rape, arson, treason, criminal acts of inferior justices, and crimes against widows and orphans, could also be processed by the audiencia in the first instance.[5] Such judicial responsibilities were extremely important by themselves. When compared to the political functions of the court, however, it becomes obvious the audiencia was an important political institution. In the viceregal capital it served as the viceroy's council of state. All major decisions or departures from established procedures required the agreement of the oidores of the audiencia. The *acuerdo* (agreement) of the judges served as an interim ruling on the constitutionality of the viceroy's actions. Only a politically naive viceroy failed to value the audiencia's support. In the case of a viceroy's death, and in the absence of any instructions to the contrary, the court assumed supreme executive authority.[6] As has been noted, the audiencia served the crown's political objectives in a very effective manner. Its political success could not be denied. A seventeenth-century jurist, Juan de Solórzano Pereira, very aptly characterized the audiencias throughout the empire as "the foundation and defense of those kingdoms . . ." and continuing in a less exact fashion, "where justice is done, where the poor are defended from the oppression of the great and powerful, and where every man may claim his own in truth and in law."[7] Unfortunately, the political success of the court contrasted sharply with its judicial failure.

Evolution of Viceregal Judicial Structure

In 1535, with the appointment of Antonio de Mendoza as first viceroy of New Spain, the audiencia relinquished its position at the apex of the political structure, theoretically enabling the court to devote more attention to its judicial duties.

The audiencia, however, found it difficult to function in the newly pacified kingdom. Common sense demanded a quick response from Spanish officials faced with the necessity of impressing conquered Indians with their political control and its corollary—the enforcement of order. To have requested permission from the court before executing sentence, as technically required, would delay—perhaps dangerously—the demonstration of Spanish authority. Consequently, the court's judicial powers were suspended, allowing local officials to execute sentences immediately, without prior approval of the high court. Normal judicial procedure remained suspended until 1601, when the audiencia resumed its legal functions. The uncertain state of order, however, resulted in a further suspension from 1664 to 1695. A major judicial responsibility of the audiencia thus remained suspended for most of the period between 1535 and 1695.[8]

The suspension of the audiencia's authority over sentences imposed by inferior magistrates resulted in a further subordination of its judicial duties to its active political responsibilities. Even under normal circumstances the judges of the criminal sala, in keeping with the importance placed on political functions, did not enjoy the higher status accorded the civil judges, the oidores.[9] The morale of the alcaldes del crimen suffered and the sala became hopelessly corrupt and inefficient. Minor functionaries kept the sala operating in a perfunctory manner, while the judges themselves did scarcely more than receive their salaries. Routine police patrols within the district of the viceregal capital, although a responsibility of the criminal chamber, were seldom made on a regular basis.[10]

While the audiencia engrossed in its political duties offered little assistance in maintaining order, other royal officials were equally as ineffective and for the same reason; the subordination of judicial responsibilities to political duties. The corregidor, who functioned as a district political officer, automatically became a member of the municipal council in the city or town of his residence, representing the king. His political duties overshadowed all other responsibilities, although as a judicial officer he shared the responsibility of maintaining civil order—apprehending and sentencing malefactors. Another crown official, the alcalde mayor, possessed much the same responsibilities of the corregidor exercising both political and judicial duties.[11] The only judicial officials relieved of pressing political responsibilities were the municipal magistrates. The ordinary magistrates of the city council (*jueces ordinarios*) were not crown officers and, although not entirely free of political duties, their main functions were judicial.

Unfortunately, municipal magistrates, while free of the political preoccupations of crown officials, could not be relied on to bear the burden of law enforcement. Territorially restricted to their districts, they proved no match against bandits who crossed into other jurisdictions to avoid capture. Local judges, selected from respected residents by the council for a one-year term, lacked professional interest in law enforcement, accepting the post more for the status that it conferred than from a sense of civic responsibility.[12] These judges, in small urban centers in particular, inclined toward a paternalistic approach to law enforcement, an attitude that preserved a reasonable degree of local harmony at the expense of the exact observance of the laws. Solórzano Pereira, referring to the local magistrates, noted with disapproval that "only rarely is justice carried out completely and without restraint."[13]

Agents of the corregidor or alcalde mayor and municipal police officers patrolled the urban centers and their outlying districts. In Mexico City and Guadalajara (seat of the separate audiencia of the kingdom of New Galicia) agents of the sala del crimen also made rounds, delivering those picked up directly to the alcaldes of the sala. In the viceregal capital a corp of watchmen, the *guarda de pito* also bore limited responsibility for apprehending malefactors in addition to assisting the inhabitants in case of fire or personal emergency.[14] A criminal in the capital might be arrested by any one of several authorities. Rather than leading to coordinated law enforcement, the situation often caused quarrels over who should sentence the offender. Solórzano Pereira felt that such squabbles could best be dealt with by suppressing municipal magistrates in cities or towns where a corregidor or alcalde mayor resided. In 1783 a more rational system of deploying law enforcement personnel in the the capital would be made possible by the division of the city into eight principal districts (*cuarteles*) subdivided into thirty-two smaller units.[15] Such a system permitted the assignment of specified individuals in one particular area, focusing both their efforts and responsibilities. While authorities hailed the step as an important move to make enforcement more efficient, the old problem of overlapping jurisdictions remained.

Complementing this essentially Spanish system of justice was a separate Indian judicial structure. The placing of limited judicial power in the hands of the native inhabitants was inspired by Spain's willingness to recognize the authority of Indian nobles, the caciques, when it did not conflict with the crown's sovereignty. Spain preferred not to see itself as a usurper. Rather, control of Indian communities could best be accomplished through Indian officials under the watchful eyes of a Spanish corregidor or alcalde mayor. Initially the caciques exercised the authority of a *gobernador* (governor) with virtually the same political and judicial responsibilities of a corregidor. The idea of political power vested in a hereditary nobility, even an Indian one, was, however, basically repugnant to the crown and in violation of its already well-established policy of making political power dependent on royal appointments rather than inherited feudal rights. As a consequence, a royal cédula in 1538 ordered the election of Indian gobernadores who would also be invested with the functions of a cacique thus moving toward a nonheriditary Indian officialdom.[16] In 1549 the crown required Indian communities to choose their own municipal officials, governing themselves along the same lines as a Spanish municipality, electing councilmen (*regidores*) and municipal magistrates as well as the standard assortment of town functionaries.[17] It became the responsibility of these Indian officials to administer justice in a manner consistent with Spanish practices. The audiencia exercised the usual appellate functions, hearing cases in the second instance, as well as approving major penalties imposed by Indian officials. Around 1573 a special tribual, the *juzgado general de indios*, was established by the audiencia to hear appeals from the acts of corregidores and alcaldes mayores in cases involving Indians.[18]

A system of justice formulated more to further the political objectives of the crown than to facilitate the ordering of society was only viable in a static situation. The relatively simple society of the first half century of conquest required a minimum of European judicial intervention. The Indian social structure did not collapse after 1521 but continued to function. Indian officials, acting in accordance with native tradition and norms, maintained order with little difficulty. An orderly Indian society permitted the crown to devote its energy to the more pressing problem of establishing royal authority in New Spain. Events indeed justified the crown's political preoccupations. The judicial system, designed to protect royal prerogatives, failed to adjust to the needs of a more varied situation as the society of conquest evolved. The rapidly growing number of mestizos and other racial mixtures, without a secure position in society, because of their mixed parentage, added a complex element to the previously simple division between the conquerors and the conquered. Such groups were not governed by an automatic allegiance to either Indian or European values but would develop their own norms to reflect social reality. The growth of a disorderly group of Spanish vagabonds further complicated the adminstration of order. Not being skilled artsisans or suitable for positions in the expanding viceregal government, such people failed to find the opportunities they had expected. Even the need for unskilled labor could be adequately filled by the Indian population. Unable to fit into the Spanish economy at any level, they were content to live a parasitic existence among the Indians, using their undefined status as Spaniards to require goods and services from the confused villagers. Small groups of vagabonds moved across the kingdom of New Spain, corrupting Indian customs and imposing their will on a society still awed by the conquest.[19] Moreover, the concentration of economic power in principal urban centers made it difficult to build a network of viable towns. Rural inhabitants drifted from their marginal communities into the cities only to find the attractions of city life more myth than reality. Crime and frustration became part of their urban existence.[20]

In 1553, trying to cope with increasing disorder, the crown attempted to establish the santa hermanded in New Spain to assist in maintaining order. Whether due to lack of qualified residents or for unknown reasons, the organization did not prove a success.[21] In 1631 the crown once again attempted to establish the hermandad in the Indies. To add to its prestige the office was made part of the municipal council, with "voz y voto" and the position equivalent to an alcalde mayor. In the absence of an *alcalde provincial*, the jurisdiction of the hermandad could legally be exercised by the *alcalde ordinario*.[22] The office of the provincial of the hermandad thus became closely identified with the municipal council, and it was precisely this close connection that weakened the office. The duties of the provincial of the hermandad became submerged in the many other responsibilities of the municipal council. Thus, the hermandad's special jurisdiction remained ineffective in New Spain.

The ability of the viceregal judicial structure to maintain order weakened when Indian society began to deteriorate as a consequence of the introduction of European epidemic disease. The great epidemics of 1576 and 1579, smallpox and measles in particular, virtually decimated the hapless Indian population.[23] New Spain entered the seventeenth century still staggering from these demographic disasters. The Indian gradually acquired a degree of immunity and began a slow recovery. A population decline of such magnitude, however, necessitated social and economic adjustments by every class and caste.

The demand for Indian labor to meet the expanding economy of New Spain far exceeded the number of laborers readily available, causing both economic problems and social tension. The shortage of Indian labor resulted in active competition among employers to secure an adequate labor force. By 1627 the labor demands of the viceregal government could be met only with difficulty. It became necessary to draft Indians from towns and villages outside the valley of Mexico to meet governmental labor requirements. Textile factories (*obrajes*), which had always experienced difficulty in holding their labor force because of bad treatment and hard work, turned to convict labor. Local officials imposed obraje sentences for a variety of crimes, often in cooperation with factory owners. Even Indian officials, formerly exempt from forced labor, were pressed into the labor market. The critical shortage broke down Indian class distinctions, reducing all Indians to the same level.[24] Increasing pressure forced many Indians to seek the protection of willing landholders, who incorporated them into their labor pool. Such rural labor, in spite of many drawbacks, was more acceptable and in line with Indian traditions than labor in factories, mines, or public works. Nor were mestizos immune from the voracious demand for labor, although they could aspire to a more exalted status as foremen or supervisors of Indian labor. Such significant social changes could not be accomplished without bitterness and violence. Temporary vagrancy and vice were natural consequences of the time.

Difficulty in obtaining labor seriously affected food production. To further complicate the situation, European landholders had taken advantage of demographic changes to acquire uninhabited or sparsely populated Indian land. The incorporation of such land into the Spanish haciendas resulted in inefficient land use and the inadequate production of foodstuffs. If the Indians had previously only managed to scrape a subsistence living from the land, they had at least sustained themselves. The loss of Indian land coupled with population recovery began to strain available food supplies. For the first time cities faced food shortages and rising prices of basic commodities. As early as 1578, the viceregal government established a state granary in Mexico City to stabilize prices of basic cereals and meet emergencies.[25] Significantly, the first large scale riot occurred in Mexico City in 1624 occasioned by food shortages and rising prices.[26] After 1631 Mexico City lived under the constant threat of famine.[27] Such a state of affairs made the maintenance of order a difficult task. The marginal existence of most of the population could easily be imperiled by shortages and the upward movement of prices. Under these circumstances, banditry or some other form of irregular behavior became the only alternative to starvation.

Although the non-European elements of the population undoubtedly suffered more than the more privileged European class, criminal behavior was not restricted to one color or caste. Diarist Antonio de Robles noted the whipping and hanging of Spaniards and creoles, as well as Indians and mestizos.[28] The Italian traveler Gemelli Carreri reported seeing over four hundred prisoners, of every race and mixture, all originally seized for theft or robbery during a viceregal prison inspection.[29] Penalties, in keeping with European standards of justice, were severe. Whipping regardless of sex was common, and hanging or physical mutilation was frequently the sentence in robbery cases without regard for color or caste. Simple vagrancy was often harshly dealt with in order to provide a public example. Carreri observed the punishment of three women accused of vagrancy who not only were publicly whipped but also taken underneath the gallows, covered with syrup and feathered.[30] Exemplary justice, however, had little deterrent effect given the precarious economic position of the majority of the population. The uneasy state of order could rapidly deteriorate into violence. An extreme example of such deterioration occurred in the last decade of the century.

During the course of an extremely wet summer in 1691, marked by extensive flooding and destruction in the valley of Mexico, worms attacked the crops. The resultant small summer harvest forced prices up and brought hunger and death throughout New Spain. The state granary quickly became the main source of cereals. To add to the plight of the hungry people, severe weather caused meager winter and spring harvests.[31] Bread became impossible to obtain in Mexico City, and by January of the following year, meat was in short supply. Tension between Europeans and Indians mounted as wheat-eating Spaniards and creoles turned to the Indian staple of maize, further restricting the supply and driving the price upward. The build-up of racial strife could only have been further inflamed by an edict prohibiting priests from administering the communion wafer to Indians presumably because of the shortage of wheat.[32]

The inevitable explosion occurred on Sunday, June 8, 1692. A mob of Indians, bearing the body of a man allegedly killed by two mestizo employees of the state granary, gathered in front of the archbishop's residence demanding justice. Unfortunately, the bishop could not be located and an aide referred the Indians to the viceregal palace. When the mob arrived at the palace, the viceroy was also unavailable. A small group of Indians, refusing to accept the fact, stoned the palace gates. Under such provocation the palace guard unwisely sallied forth and drove the crowd away from the plaza, but immediately more Indians joined the mob, forcing the guardsmen to flee to the safety of the palace courtyard. The now inflamed Indians attempted to storm the viceregal palace, touching off the worst civil disorder in Mexican colonial history. The riot, in which all racial groups of the population participated, resulted in the partial destruction of the viceregal palace and other public buildings, as well as the extensive looting of stores and warehouses located in the vicinity of the palace.[33]

A wave of fear and distrust, directed mainly at the Indians, in spite of the fact that other elements played a prominent role in the looting, swept the capital. The government banned the sale of pulque and ordered Indians to remain within their own districts, prohibiting gatherings of more than five people. Repeated rumors of hostile Indians approaching the city caused panic among the European elements. A riot occurred in Guadalajara, and a full-scale uprising in Tlaxcala prompted the immediate dispatch of troops to restore order.[34] Those unlucky enough to be apprehended by the authorities received harsh punishment. A mestizo, alleged to have set fire to the public gallows during the riot, was ordered burned in front of the newly reconstructed gallows. Three Indians accused of setting fire to the viceregal palace were shot and their hands severed and displayed on sticks at the palace gates. Lesser offenders of both sexes endured public whipping.[35] Such actions restored a measure of order in Mexico City, although food shortages continued well into the next year.

The underlying causes of the violence were not readily understood. The wide difference between the life style of the rich and the abject poverty of the poor appeared to be a wholly natural phenomenon of life, requiring only the giving of alms by the wealthy to help alleviate the wretched condition of the lower classes. Alms giving, while not insignificant, could not alter the situation. Many monasteries and convents distributed food, and the viceroy and the archbishop, on special occasions, lavished alms on the poor.[36] But distribution of food by the religious orders faced curtailment as supplies became scarce, and individual generosity, while commendable, was of little permanent help to the poverty stricken. One educated observer reported that the reason for the violent outburst in 1692 was generally held to be God's punishment for sins committed, and the morally weak Indian element of the population was his instrument.[37]

Although the riot of 1692 would never again be equaled in intensity in colonial Mexico, partly because of its improving economy as New Spain slowly came out of what has been described as a "century of depression," the maintenance of order continued to be a problem. The slim margin between starvation and the subsistence living of a large segment of the population reinforced the already well-established tendency toward vagrancy and crime.

Vagrancy became a permanent feature of colonial life from the sixteenth century through the eighteenth.[38] Gemelli Carreri observed that vagrants were a constant threat to the security of property—breaking through tile roofs or burning down heavy wooden doors to sack houses and stores. Even the more favored classes found it difficult to avoid the depredations of the dispossessed. Thieves set fire to the coach house of the secretary of the sala del crimen, after stripping the building of anything of value, and then had the audacity to make their getaway in the unfortunate secretary's coaches. Even the viceroy's personal staff did not escape attention; thieves robbed the viceroy's doctor of over 5,000 pesos worth of worked silver. Skillfully disguised, such stolen articles could be sold at bargain prices at the *baratillo* or thieves market, which in the seventeenth century was located in the central plaza.[39]

Nor was life or property more secure in rural areas. Bandits literally inundated the entire viceroyalty, restricting communication between population centers. The uncertain state of order affected trade and commerce and threatened to cut off the major cities, making them islands in the midst of a sea of banditry. In Mexico City the unscheduled return of a carriage with the blinds drawn signified that bandits had stopped the carriage, removing, as customary, even the clothes of their unfortunate victims.[40]

The inefficient judicial structure, with the sala del crimen at its highest level, appeared unable to cope with the disorders brought about by far-reaching changes in colonial society. The ineffectiveness of the judicial system at such a critical moment magnified the degree of disorder in the viceroyalty. The crown, rather than face the problem, attributed the disorders to the many mixtures and races in the population of New Spain. The inhabitants of the viceroyalty were accused of having a natural propensity for violence and disorder. Undoubtedly, maintaining order in the colony was more difficult than it was in Spain; many of the king's New World subjects were not philosophically attuned to the Spanish judicial system. A large number, on the very fringes of Spanish culture or even beyond its influence, had no active contact with the law. Mexico had all the problems encountered in a frontier region. Even in areas under direct Spanish control, a progressive deterioration of order could be observed. The disturbances arising from significant social changes and the marginal existence of a hard-pressed population obviously would have taxed even the most efficient and dedicated colonial administration. The failure of the system, however, was not a simple matter of an inefficient judicial structure being overwhelmed by a rapidly mounting crime rate. The problem lay in a defective institutional structure that made it difficult to organize the power of the government to maintain order in an increasingly complex society.

Neither justice nor order could adequately be served by existing judicial organizations. To revitalize a judicial system that had never actually functioned presented a major problem. Viceroy Linares, although unable to reform the system, at least recognized the need for action. His successor, the Marqués de Valero, instead of attempting to inject some life into the existing judicial structure, established the tribunal of the acordada, a new and independent organization to administer criminal justice. By establishing the acordada the viceroy neatly sidestepped the problem of restructuring the regular judicial system, thus avoiding a political confrontation with the audiencia. Turning to a historical precedent, the marquis built the new judicial institution around the old jurisdiction of the hermandad. The hermandad, with its historical roots in the failure of the regular authorities to maintain order, appeared to be an ideal solution to rescue the viceroyalty from approaching anarchy.

Events—more than a sense of history—dictated the Marqués de Valero's choice of the hermandad as the core of the new judicial organization. In 1710, at the request of the inhabitants of Querétaro, Miguel Velázquez de Lorea received an appointment as an alcalde provincial of the hermandad.[41] Velázquez quickly set about the task of restoring order around the city of Querétaro, demonstrating a rare combination of zeal and energy which soon attracted the favorable attention of the viceroy. Subsequently, the marquis requested Velázquez to dislodge a gang of bandits from a hacienda in the vicinity of Valladolid. Velázquez apparently protested that he would not carry out the order unless permitted to execute sentences also. Viceroy Valero promptly conceded the necessary powers, and the bandits met their end on improvised gallows—the nearest tree.[42]

Such methods, while effective, were extralegal. Consequently,

Evolution of Viceregal Judicial Structure

in order to regularize Velazquez's labors without inhibiting his efficiency, Valero used the tribunal of the acordada. Meeting with the audiencia in consultative session, the viceroy made Velázquez's sentences final and exempted him from reporting his sentences to the sala del crimen.[43] This decision was made *con acuerdo* (with agreement) of the audiencia, and hence the name "acordada." The crown approved the viceroy's actions in 1722, appointing Miguel Velázquez the first proprietary judge and captain of the acordada.[44]

The zeal and energy of Miguel Velázquez soon became legendary. Riding at the head of his men, the judge of the acordada terrorized the bandits who had so recently enjoyed almost uncontested freedom. Acting with cold efficiency, Velázquez hunted down offenders, sentenced them, and carried out executions within minutes of their capture. The grim evidence was left hanging from a tree as a warning to anyone similarly inclined. Velázquez's methods soon managed to turn the tide of lawlessness to favor the established authorities. It was only necessary to unfurl the standard of the acordada in front of a column in order to guarantee its safety from bandits.

The tremendous odds against Velázquez's success lent a distinct aura of romance to his many feats. Among the numerous bandits who fell before Velázquez's sword, the most remarkable was a group bent on robbery on the grand scale. The bandits had boldly planned to march on Mexico City, seize the royal arsenal, and storm the treasury, using the captured weapons to reduce the palace guard. Fortunately, news of the plans reached the viceroy, who immediately ordered the acordada to break up the gang. Velázquez managed to destroy their dreams at the end of a rope.[45] Even on his deathbed Miguel Velázquez thought only of duty. In the last hours of his life he reportedly arranged the sentencing of some prisoners, at which time his confessor admonished him to forget such things and concentrate on asking for God's mercy. Velázquez replied that the obligations of justice must never be forgotten.[46]

In 1732 José Velázquez succeeded his father as proprietary judge of the acordada and continued to add to its by now lengendary reputation. The notorious Pedro Razo who had held the province of Zacatecas in mortal terror, was soon brought to heel.[47] The equally infamous *Celayenses* literally went down before his sword.

José Velázquez had the leader's head cut off and taken to Celaya for public display.[48] On his death, the younger Velázquez was eulogized as the David who had restored peace to Judea and Israel.[49]

Subsequent judges of the acordada added to the legends, and their feats entered into the songs of the people. When judge Santa María captured the bandit Piedra y Paredes, a popular song recorded his success as follows:

> Señor Santa María
> has to build a house
> he already has stone and walls (Piedra y Paredes)
> now he only lacks wood (Madera).[50]

In addition to the remarkable deeds of the judges and the judicial efficiency of the acordada, the fact that those who fell into its hands seemed to disappear from the face of the earth added an air of mystery and terror to the tribunal. Those held by the tribunal keenly felt their plight and isolation from society. An obviously well-educated prisoner compared his situation to that of Christians held captive by the Moors who had recourse only to God, being denied all else.[51] The tribunal itself attempted to cultivate this emotional reaction, which made its duties less difficult; at the entrance to the prison of the acordada, engraved in royal octaves, a general warning read:

> Passerby, be wary of this place
> and see that you avoid entering
> since once its hard doors close
> only for your execution will they open.[52]

During its existence the tribunal processed over 62,900 prisoners, executing 888 and sentencing 19,410 to presidio terms.[53]

The tribunal of the acordada, although created under social stress, represented a basic philosophical departure in colonial government. As a new institution, formed in the New World to meet the particular needs of the viceroyalty of New Spain, it was unique. The tribunal was not a transplanted Spanish institution but a major innovation of the colonial bureaucracy. The acordada, moreover, was the only tribunal in the viceroyalty of New Spain with unlimited territorial jurisdiction, encompassing not only the kingdom of New Spain but the dependent kingdoms of New Galicia and

New Vizcaya. Only the viceroy had the same jurisdiction and he, unlike the judge of the acordada, worked through a large viceregal administration, two audiencias (one in Mexico City and the other in Guadalajara), and various provincial governors. The acordada, however, was controlled from Mexico City by a judge independent of all territorial governors and judicial bodies, including the two audiencias of Mexico and Guadalajara. Unlike the viceroy, who could not remove royal appointees without permission of the crown, the judge of the acordada could extend and recall commissions at his pleasure. The judge answered directly to the viceroy, subordinated only to viceregal authority. The individual agents of the acordada were not limited to one territorial jurisdiction as were ordinary justices, although the laws of the Indies clearly stated the desirablity of restricted territorial jurisdictions, limiting the exercise of authority to strictly defined areas for each governor, alcalde, and other officials.[54]

Agents freely operated outside their usual districts, apprehending wrongdoers and formulating charges without hindrance from the ordinary justices in any jurisdiction. Originally restricted to rural areas, the tribunal's jurisdiction was extended by authorization of the crown in 1756 to urban centers, including Mexico City. The all-encompassing jurisdiction represented a major innovation and accounted for much of the acordada's success. Of even greater significance, the tribunal, primarily a judicial organization, was the only viceregal judicial body without political or administrative functions. Its development represented an important move toward a more rational concept of the adminstration of justice and closer to the modern ideal of a separate judiciary.

While chaotic conditions obviously forced colonial officials to create the acordada, its approval by the crown as well as the subsequent extension of its authority indicated that the tribunal fitted in with the attempts of the new Bourbon dynasty to reform Spanish administration. Whether the Hapsburg monarchs, with their historical suspicion of powerful and independent institutions, would have permitted the creation of such an organization is debatable. The tribunal of the acordada, however, impelled by the crisis in New Spain, definitely represented a new direction in the administration of justice as well as an admission by colonial authorities that the increasingly complex society of New Spain could not be satisfactorily governed without a judicial organization freed of political and administrative responsibilities.

The tribunal of the acordada became the core law enforcement organization in New Spain. Viceroys valued its services and cautioned their successors to guard the tribunal's prerogatives from the pressure of competing institutions, including the audiencia of Mexico. The oidores of the high court almost instantly regretted their agreement with the executive establishing an organization exempt from the normal supervision of the audiencia's sala del crimen. Viceroy Revilla Gigedo, who felt that the regular judicial structure had avoided its responsibilities, maintained that the acordada processed four-fifths of all criminal cases in the viceroyalty.[55] While the viceroy's estimate cannot be substantiated, it is clear that colonial administrators viewed the tribunal as the single most important enforcement agency in New Spain. The fact that the acordada was subject only to viceregal supervision partially explains the attitude of the government. Most viceroys, with the notable exception of Revilla Gigedo, characterized the organization as a reliable arm of colonial administration free of the restrictions that circumscribed the activities of traditional judicial authorities.

The ability of the acordada to move decisively, without being unduly hampered by regulations, obviously appealed to those responsible for the conservation of the viceroyalty. At the same time, the initial absence of restrictions and control over the tribunal could not be accepted by the oidores and others committed to traditional legal procedures sanctified by Spanish law and the extensive legal tradition of Iberian jurisprudence. Inevitably, the acordada clashed with the other judicial authorities. The wide jurisdiction of the tribunal brought it into contact with all levels of the judicial structure and society. To local landholders and merchants, often themselves involved in the volunteer activities of the tribunal, as well as to members of the lower classes and the criminal elements, the acordada represented viceregal law and order. Like all other judicial bodies, the tribunal operated in accordance with the social expectations and norms established by colonial society. Varying standards of behavior, shaped by class and racial attitudes, influenced the tribunal's operation and determined which groups received the protection of the laws and which were identified as potentially deviant elements to be controlled.

3 CRIMINALITY IN THE SOCIAL CONTEXT OF NEW SPAIN

Modern criminology suggests that the entire social order is composed of various conflict patterns. The legal system then adjusts conflicting interests on the basis of the relative power of individual groups. As a natural consequence, the laws tend to become increasingly punitive when applied to less powerful classes. Such a tendency is important in maintaining and enhancing the power of those in authority. Criminality hence becomes a question of social status defined by how members of a particular class are perceived by those in power. Deviant behavior is associated with certain classes while at the same time the causal factors tend to be forgotten. The expectations of the authorities then are that certain groups will act in a way characteristically viewed as undesirable and potentially deviant.[1] Such an overall theory appears to be applicable to New Spain.

As has been demonstrated, the Iberian legal tradition cannot be separated from the political evolution of the Castilian monarchy. Varying penalties together with special privileges, depending on an individual's position in society, were a feature of Spanish codes as well as many other contemporary codes. One of the major aims of nineteenth-century Spanish liberalism would be to eliminate the special fueros that institutionalized the uneven application of the laws.[2]

Numerous examples of varying penalties may be found in the *Novísima recopilación de las leyes de España* (1805). A law (1734) setting sentences in cases involving theft in Madrid and its surrounding area imposed capital punishment on all offenders. A member of the nobility, however, accused of such a crime, avoided the loss of status associated with the public hanging accorded common criminals by being condemned to be executed by garroting, a form of capital punishment deemed more in keeping with his rank.[3] In cases of minor importance such as the theft in the streets of capes, mantillas, or other items of dress, which did not necessitate breaking and entering, another law (1745) was promulgated. It clarified and reduced the penalties imposed by the *pragmática* referred to above. It also provided for a mandatory sentence of 200 lashes, ten years in the galleys, and branding with the letter "L" for *ladrón* (thief) in the case of commoners. Nobles accused of the identical crime avoided branding as well as a public flogging. In addition the law provided for two possible penalties, depending on the circumstances, rather than the single mandatory sentence imposed on those of common origins.[4]

The *Recopilación de leyes de los reynos de las Indias* (1791) provides another example. Indian caciques, theoretically incorporated into the hidalguía, received treatment in keeping with their social standing. Ordinary judges could not apprehend a cacique except in the case of an extremely serious offense and in such an instance had to immediately advise the audiencia.[5]

The crown demonstrated its concern for the preservation of a hierarchical society in an attempt to legislate against unequal marriages. A decree in 1776 required parental consent to a marriage until the son or daughter reached the age of twenty-five to assure that puerile romance did not result in undesirable alliances. Those who ignored the law not only had to deal with familial wrath but also faced legal disinheritance. In Spanish America the pragmática applied to all classes and races with the exception of mulattoes, blacks, coyotes, and others of "similar origins."[6] The parental consent law considered Indian caciques, in defiance of social reality but in keeping with political theory and objectives, in the same category as distinguished Spaniards. Such a decree could not be enforced except on a very selective basis; nevertheless. it represented an important philosophical and political statement. Clearly, Spanish law recognized the existence of classes as well as their relative power and the interests of the crown in supporting the position of one class over another.

In Spain's American empire the connection between class and crime became a fixed tenet of the judicial philosophy which conditioned the response of the authorities to crime. Viceroy Revilla

Gigedo, the elder, reported that the lower classes on the whole suffered from "evil inclinations" and a natural propsensity for vice and disorder.[7] Viewing the viceroyalty's inhabitants, especially those of mixed racial origins, as being unable to understand or appreciate the need for order, colonial authorities appeared prepared to tolerate a high level of criminal behavior, although such expectations were not necessarily fulfilled. Consequently, a degree of "normal" antisocial behavior among the various castes of New Spain could be excused by colonial officials. Such views governed the thinking of the colonial bureaucracy from the first to the last century of Spanish rule. The Council of the Indies, the highest level of colonial administration, noted that one could not compare the racially mixed inhabitants of the Indies to the simple people in Spain, because, unlike those in the mother country, they possessed "vicious origins and nature."[8] Official sentiments along these lines conditioned judicial authorities charged with maintaining law and order in the multiracial society of New Spain.

Viceregal officials applied these sentiments to every color and caste, including the creoles—those born of European parents in the New World. While the Spanish-American creole could hardly have been considered a vile and base mixture, his personality, formed in the colony, was deemed to be different from that of a native-born Spaniard. Supposedly, the creole suffered from such personality defects as impulsiveness, excessive pride, and irresponsibility, as well as from a weakened sense of morals. A penniless immigrant from the mother country considered himself morally superior to those Europeans unfortunate enough to have been born in New Spain. Colonial society supported this preposterous contention to the extent of indulging in all sorts of euphemisms to avoid the social stigma associated with an American birth. In the eighteenth century the creole became a victim of a theory maintaining that because the New World appeared to be of recent origins its plant and animal life had not matured; consequently, more advanced strains introduced into the hemisphere inevitably degenerated. The product of such a process could only be inferior.[9] The Mexican pamphleteer and author José Joaquín Fernández de Lizardi brilliantly portrayed the life of one of these degenerated and weak-willed characters in his novel *Don Catrín de la Fachenda* (*Mr. Dandy the Showoff*). His central character plunges through a series of adventures reaching ever lower depths. Don Catrín, born into a good family, viewed work as unworthy of his ancestry and, as a consequence, attempted to live by his wits—a decision that resulted in a rapid descent through the roles of soldier, swindler, gambler, comedian, servant in a brothel, assailant, and beggar.[10]

Although the creole was considered socially inferior, the government could not openly express such a prejudice. The European of American birth filled an important role in the economy in the middle and lower ranges of the colonial government, also providing a strong cultural link that bound the colonies to the mother country. The discrimination and prejudice directed toward the creole tended to be more subtle than that officially sanctioned and openly practiced against other racial groups.

Unlike the creole, the Indians' socially inferior position was reinforced by law. The paternalistic attitude of the crown, reflected in legislation, inevitably undermined the Indians' social position. Taking into account that the aboriginal inhabitants of the New World could not immediately conform to Spanish norms, the laws made the Indian a legal minor, entitled to the special protection of the crown. The long range objective was to elevate them to a level where they could appreciate the reason and justness of European laws and procedures. The classification of Indians as *gente sin razón*, which was initially intended to indicate their distance from the norms of Spanish culture and not their intellectual potential, nevertheless provided much of the philosophical justification for the exploitation of the Indian from colonial times to the present. Their alleged ignorance or lack of reason made crimes perpetrated by Indians a type of juvenile offense almost to be expected. Such crimes obviously could not be regarded with the same degree of seriousness as criminal acts engaged in by socially responsible Spaniards.

The low expectations of judicial authorities also encouraged mestizos, mulattoes, and other racial mixtures to perform antisocial acts. The law, however, did not accord the racially mixed inhabitants of New Spain apprenticeship status as it did the Indian. Although these various peoples were expected to engage in a high degree of "normal" criminal activity because of their alleged character deficiencies, once the legal machinery of the viceroyalty was forced into action against them, punishment tended to be harsh. Since the authorities viewed them as naturally vicious people who could not be redeemed by time and legal apprenticeship as could the Indian, the only alternative appeared to be severe exemplary justice. Judicial officials considered mestizos and other mixtures as potential if not actual criminals. Bartolomé de Góngora's book, *El corregidor sagaz* (1656), noted such expectations in the story of Don Juan Pareja who, amazed to come across a white-haired and aged mulatto, concluded that he must be a saint since he had reached such an advanced age without being stabbed or hanged.[11] While Góngora's mulatto and Fernández de Lizardi's unfortunate hero obviously portrayed stereotypes, such conceptions determined handling of law enforcement.

In a society officially viewed as composed of naturally vicious and criminally inclined inhabitants and Indians in a state of perpetual social apprenticeship, the legal structure could hardly function as it did in Spain. The low esteem in which the colonial administration held the population conditioned these officials to expect very little in the way of conformity to European standards of behavior. They consequently adjusted the outer limits of acceptable behavior to fit the imagined character of the inhabitants. Such an approach encouraged a paternalistic ad hoc enforcement of order without reference to specific laws or standard judicial procedures. Provincial administrators, such as alcaldes mayores, corregidores and, later their replacements, the intendents and *subdelegados*, had wide discretion in handling disorders without involving the judicial machinery.

According to testimony of a subdelegado, a man with thirty-nine years of service among the Indians of New Spain as an alcalde mayor and corregidor, in addition to service as a judge of residencia, there would not be sufficient time or personnel to process all those arrested in village brawls if the local officials brought the cases to a superior authority. He also confirmed the practice of governing the indigenous population like children, disciplining them without the necessity of formal judgments or procedures.[12] The Indian, only able to influence in a negative sense the formation of the norms subscribed to by colonial society, accepted the paternalistic administration of criminal justice. Such acceptance stemmed in part from the fact that it provided a feasible and workable accomodation between the objectives of European laws and the reality of life on the fringes of Spanish culture. Punishment meted out by local officials seemed preferable to becoming enmeshed in a judicial system dominated by Spaniards and not particularly trusted or understood by the Indians. In addition, local punishment tended to be immediate and of short duration.

The same willingness to submit to paternalistic law enforcement was present among the other castes of New Spain. To become entangled in the judicial system without power or influence, where the very membership in a certain class or racial group indicated a propensity for criminal behavior, made the question of justice irrelevant in the face of social reality. Local disturbances often warranted a mere night in jail followed the next morning by an admission of guilt and a humble request for forgiveness. More serious crimes, such as robbery or assault, could also be settled in an informal manner. The essential condition of local control was the extension of pardon by the offended party and restitution of stolen property. In cases involving physical harm the delinquent paid the victim's medical expenses.[13]

The regular judicial system came into play only when a case involved a serious crime that merited a public display of judicial authority. Most cases actually processed according to the law resulted from formal denunciation not only of the crime itself but the alleged perpetrator as well. Such a process in effect challenged judicial officials to display their legal authority. Passive law enforcement, however, did not extend to criminal activity that threatened the maintenance of political control. Banditry, or other criminal activities that appeared to have reached a dangerous degree of virulence, imperiled governmental authority and damaged the confidence of the population in the ultimate ability of the viceroyal government to control society within acceptable limits. Consequently, the authorities were capable of an immediate and active response when the situation warranted it; the acordada itself had been formed to meet such a need for energetic enforcement.

Many who fell into the official arms of the law already had been identified as recidivists.[14] Despite an obvious predisposition to assume the guilt of an accused, especially since denunciation was so heavily relied upon, judicial officers collected formal proof against an offender. A significant number of cases were dismissed as unsubstantiated. Such a conclusion did not, however, result in a suspect being declared innocent. In fact, documentation reveals a considerable reluctance to extend any such doubts in favor of the accused. The decision to release a prisoner because of lack of evidence often noted that in any event he had spent a period of time, often in excess of a year, in custody.[15] Thus, if the guilty party escaped his just due, he had at least suffered partial punishment. He generally began the process identified as criminally inclined and finished with his criminal status either confirmed or still suspected, but never cleared.

Although the system reflected the viceroyal government's lack of confidence in the mixed population of New Spain, it was not necessarily oppressive. Innocent people could, and undoubtedly did, become involved with judicial officials with unfortunate results. Several factors, however, countered the possibility of any significant number of innocent individuals being processed through the judicial machinery. Most individuals who found themselves involved in formal proceedings already had established reputations within their own class and society as malefactors. Thus, actual guilt of the crime that resulted in their imprisonment appeared to be a moot point, regarded as such by their peers. If judicial institutions had engulfed a large number of people held to be innocent by their class or society as a whole, pressure would have developed for an adjustment. That colonial officials responded to such social pressures is indicated by their adherence to procedure, even in cases involving those on the lower levels of the social system when the state imposed legal punishment. Society, including Indians and the other less favored elements of the population, demanded a degree of predictability when the state brought its formal authority to bear on the individual. The viceregal government felt constrained to meet these expectations in spite of viewing certain classes and castes virtually as born criminals. As modern criminologists have suggested, due process, in any society, is never a gift but a concesssion to the relative power of the various sectors of the population.[16]

Even at the local level the paternalistic justice administered could not be arbitrarily based on whim. Obviously, such officials had considerable latitude, since speedy and local punishment was to be preferred in most cases; however, they also faced the task of administering their districts. Such responsibility could not be satisfactorily met without the cooperation of the inhabitants.[17] Simple coercion, over an extended period, would not be feasible. A rough consensus had to be developed so that the actions of local officials including those involving punishment, fell within acceptable limits. On the formal level, colonial officials conceded due process, in spite of the expense and the imagined character of the inhabitants, because without that important concession, the social cooperation necessary to enable the state to impose its authority could not have been elicited.

The classes that were most involved in judicial procedures may be determined by statistics maintained by the sala del crimen and the acordada. The records also reveal just how much the society of castes had disintegrated. By the eighteenth century actual class standing no longer depended on race to the same extent that it had in the preceding centuries. Creoles, mestizos, mulattoes, and Indians could all be found in the lower classes, and even individuals of mixed ancestry could be found in the more favored classes. Race therefore provides only a partial gauge to an individual's class, although those of European origin obviously still dominated the upper ranges of society. The general tendency among the population in this multiracial society to pass for the most socially acceptable racial group or mixture that a person's physical characteristics allowed, further complicated the use of race to determine class.[18]

The suspect nature of all racial claims inevitably lessened the importance of race as a means of social discrimination. Judicial officers accepted a prisoner's statement as to race, unless common sense indicated otherwise. Even in such cases the records noted the person's declaration followed by the officer's remark that by his appearances he belonged to another specified racial group.[19] To more accurately place an individual in a certain class, one must also look at occupation as well as race. Both items of information appear in the records, indicating the importance placed on such data in defining a person's place within society.

A statistical sampling of 958 cases of prisoners condemned to *presidios*, the most common form of punishment resulting from formal proceedings, suggests the major racial and occupational groups that came under legal examination.[20] Spaniards, including both creoles and individuals born in the mother country, accounted for 28 percent of those receiving sentences. Of these, 28 percent fell into the artisan category, and 19 percent engaged in occupations that required some limited occupational skills but not of a level to qualify them for status of an artisan, such as coachmen, muleteers, butchers, and servants.[21] Small farmers composed 15 percent while laborers, both rural (gañán) and urban, contributed 14 percent. Small traders, minor shopkeepers and their clerks, scribes and those possessing a higher level of educational skills than other occupations required supplied 5 percent, almost balanced by 6 percent without a trade or occupation. Supervisors and overseers accounted for 4 percent while the remaining 9 percent of the cases failed to note occupation or the lack of employment. The statitics indicate that those individuals of European origins sentenced in formal judicial proceedings came from the lower class and what may be viewed as the middle sector such as artisans and small tradesmen.

Mestizos, representing 22 percent of the cases sampled, came from almost the same occupational groups as the Spaniards. Artisans comprised 31 percent, those of more limited occupational skills contributed 17 percent, small farmers made up 10 percent while laborers accounted for 20 percent. Traders and others possessing equivalent skills made up 2 percent, and individuals without trade or occupation supplied 3 percent. Those with supervisional skills contributed 4 percent and the remaining cases, 13 percent, failed to indicate occupational status. The figures suggest that the mestizos receiving presidio sentences also came from the lower and middle sector. The percentages demonstrate the progress they had achieved in working their way into a better economic situation than the other racial mixtures held under the European caste society.[22] That the mestizo had not yet attained equality with the creole is also clear from the significantly higher percentage of laborers and the lower number of traders of mestizo origin. The constant pressure applied by mestizos for a better position within the European-dominated colonial society obviously had contributed to a weakening of the caste system. The narrowing gap between the creole and the mestizo, however, owed perhaps as much to the inability of the economy of New Spain to fit a growing creole population into an economic position consistent with their alleged racial superiority. Under the circumstances, a breakdown of a system based on race into one of classes, including members of all racial elements of the population, was inevitable.[23]

The occupational groups represented by the Indians reflected their relatively lower position in society. The Indian accounted for the highest percentage of presidio sentences, 33 percent, while the number that could be considered members of the middle sector fell below that of Spaniards and mestizos. Laborers made up 30 percent followed by small farmers with 24 percent; artisans, 18 percent; supervisors, 3 percent; another 3 percent without an occupation; and an insignificant 1 percent engaged in trading or utilizing any degree of educational skills. The remaining 21 percent of the cases failed to indicate occupation or lack thereof. This high percentage may have been caused by language barriers, although Indian interpreters were supposed to be employed when necessary. It is quite possible that judicial officials, if they experienced any difficulty in eliciting such information, failed to press the matter since the individual's race sufficed to place him at the bottom or near the bottom of colonial society. Such a theory is supported by the remarkably consistent percentile of the unspecified category in the instance of the other racial elements.

The remaining major racial category, those classified as mulattoes, accounted for 17 percent of the cases sampled and shared the same low occupational status as the Indian population. Laborers composed 28 percent; small farmers, 21 percent; artisans, 19 percent; those possessing limited occupational skills, 11 percent; supervisors, 3 percent; without any occupation, 6 percent; and the remaining 12 percent listed without occupational information. Significantly no mulattoes processed fell into the more favored category of traders, scribes, and those using a degree of educational skills.

Combining the various racial categories into occupational groups, the statistics indicate that of those processed 25 percent were artisans, 23 percent laborers, 17 percent small farmers, 14 percent limited occupational skill but not of a level to qualify for the occupational status of artisans, 4 percent without any occupation, 3 percent supervisorial, another 3 percent traders and others requiring an equivalent degree of skills, and the remaining 11 percent did not note occupational status.

In view of the statistics presented, there can be little doubt that the formal judicial machinery dealt with the lower and marginally middle-class elements of society. These were the very same elements that endured the ad hoc administration of order on the local level. Law and order in New Spain reflected the relative power of the classes as well as the inevitable resort of the less favored to crime and violence, in response to the marginal position of this group within the social structure of New Spain. Race, as such, played a less important role than class in determining who became involved in the formal judicial process. Although quite obviously the bulk of the lower classes consisted of groups other than those of European origin, a significant number of cases (28 percent) involved Spaniards.

The motivation behind deviant behavior in New Spain cannot of course be determined with any degree of certainty, nevertheless one may speculate. Modern students of criminology have yet to agree on the relative importance of various factors, accepting a multiple causative theory while the process of refining continues. As far as New Spain is concerned, one can only suggest whether a particular theory has any validity. The then widely held theory of a naturally vicious people may be dismissed, at least partially, by modern man. Although colonial officials clung to such a theory to the very end, it would be a mistake to confuse it with simple bigotry.

The study of physiognomics, the relationship of the body to the mind and behavior, had developed long before the Spanish reflected on the presumed vices of their New World subjects. This line of inquiry seemed fruitful into the sixteenth and seventeenth centuries, and still is subject to periodic revival in a modified form. The Italian scientist Giambattista della Porta (1536–1615), who collected anthropometric measurements of criminals, has indeed been proposed as the first criminologist.[24] The question of the effects of physical features on man's behavior obviously occurred as Spaniards encountered new physical types among the Indians of the Americas. The idea of a natural criminally inclined mutation could be readily accepted, especially by the average Spanish settler who was predisposed to view race mixtures as inferior, and was only too willing to believe in his imagined superiority. More advanced and enlightened thought did not meet the psychological needs of the Europeans; consequently, the idea of an innately delinquent type persisted into the nineteenth century.

The effects of poverty on crime, still debated in our own century, were presented by Sir John Fortescue in the fifteenth century and vividly portrayed by Sir Thomas More and the critical Spanish philosopher Juan Luis Vives (1492–1540) in the succeeding century. Vives's description of the desperate conditions of the poor in Spain, and the vice and violence that originated from their marginal existence, would only begin to have some noticeable effect in the later decades of the eighteenth century when his work, *Tratado del socorro de los pobres*, appeared in a new edition in 1781.[25] In New Spain, where racial factors confused the question of poverty, the connection between crime and economic status proved even more difficult to accept. Society, moreover, infused with traditional religous beliefs, endowed poverty with virtues that supposedly offset its obvious drawbacks. Religious manuals described the impoverished as "poor men of Christ . . . who represent the Lord and were made poor in this world for our benefit," thus providing the more fortunate with an opportunity to exhibit Christian charity to offset some of their other spiritual shortcomings.[26] The poor, made so by divine will, could not expect anything more from society than alms. Their resort to crime in an attempt to alter their lot implied a revolt against a divinely imposed status.[27] Such an idea could not be readily accepted by society. In spite of the imagined virtues of poverty, however, many individuals of the lower classes resorted to antisocial behavior. Urban crime, undoubtedly motivated in part by the atrocious conditions of life at the bottom, was a matter of concern in all major population centers of New Spain.

If the primary economic cause of crime could be overlooked by colonial authorities, at least they recognized the connection between immediate hunger and behavior.[28] Acts of desperation motivated by severe food shortages were viewed in a different light from crime motivated by less obvious factors. Extreme hunger mitigated the seriousness of a criminal offense, although not exempting the offender from punishment. Colonial officials, attempting to avoid such situations, relied on a kingdom-wide system of granaries to supply emergency foodstuffs and hold the prices down during times of shortages. The zeal of the government stemmed in part from a keen awareness that the borderline between food riots and the loss of political control was too crucial to be ignored.

The tendency of the lower classes in New Spain to indulge in deviant activities may also have arisen from the progressive decline of Indian social values and customs and the lagging replacement of such values with those associated with European society. The weakening of aboriginal cultural norms made it difficult for the Indians to distinguish acceptable standards of conduct. Without sufficient social conditioning either from his own crumbling society or from the recently and only superficially established order approved by the Europeans, the Indian, to a certain extent, operated in a social vacuum.[29] It is also quite plausible, as Sigmund Freud proposed, that the entire process of civilization may frustrate the human animal to the point of seeking relief in antisocial behavior. To the Indian of New Spain, with his own cultural evolution broken by the Spanish conquest and faced with a new civilization of a totally different historical background and pattern, the problem of adjustment caused social uncertainty as well as tension, perhaps to the point suggested by Freud. The social problems of the Indian, who comprised an important and large segment of the colonial population, affected all elements of society.

Another theory that is of some use in considering the general impulse to engage in deviant behavior is that of defective or subverted self-concepts. Distorted social attitudes made it difficult for individuals to accomplish, or even to be accepted as worthy of filling, a legitimate social role. Such a theory may be applied to all races and mixtures including the creole, excepting only the Spaniard born in the mother country. Its degree of application would of course vary according to how those establishing the norms of society perceived the different races. Those considered naturally vile and vicious suffered more, for example, than the just slightly inferior creole. The mestizo, culturally closer to his European ancestry but placed in an inferior position because of his Indian blood, may have been the most affected. Forced by social circumstances into becoming the schemer of colonial society, the mestizo always coveted a position that matched his partial European ancestry rather than his Indian.

The Peruvian mestizo Gómez Suárez de Figueroa, better known as Garcilaso de la Vega the Inca, a name later adopted to emphasize his dual and noble ancestry, provides an excellent example of the suffering endured by his racial group throughout Spanish America. He was able to trace his ancestry on both the Indian and

Spanish side to high nobility and attempted to convince society of his right to respect. Garcilaso de la Vega contrived to elevate his Inca bloodlines to counter the idea that Indian blood served to dilute the value of his European ancestry. In his justly famous *Comentarios reales* published in two parts, the first in 1609 and the second posthumously in 1616–1617, he unavoidably demonstrated the bitterness felt by those dismissed as racially inferior. In a short chapter he insisted, perhaps too much, that while he himself proudly bore the title of mestizo, in the Spanish Indies "if a person is told: 'you're a mestizo,' or 'he's a mestizo,' it is taken as an insult."[30] De la Vega went on to note the use of the euphemistic term *montañés* by mestizos to cover the shame of their mixed origins. The only comfort available to mestizos as well as others laboring under defective self-concepts was that each racial group could look down on another and rationalize its differences in its favor. In addition, the mixed inhabitants were relied on by society to fill important roles. This softened the impact of their philosophically inferior position while perhaps heightening their frustration.

Speculation on the causes of deviant behavior in New Spain cannot be abandoned without indicating, again in a tentative fashion, the prevalence of crime. Official pronouncements concerning the level of criminal activity unfortunately do not provide a reliable guide. Often such statements were put forth to justify enlarging or continuing the activities of law enforcement agencies. The judges of the acordada, on numerous occasions, resorted to such tactics to extend or preserve their prerogatives in the face of their enemies within the viceregal government. Undoubtedly, the viceroys exaggerated criminal activity in order to provide a suitable climate for important structural changes, such as extending the tribunal of the acordada's jurisdiction into the urban centers or the division of the capital into cuarteles, or perhaps to impress upon Madrid the difficulties of governing the multiracial society of New Spain. Official statements tend to complicate the task of assessing the level of crime.

Another obvious complication is the impossibility of determining how many individuals received informal local punishment in retribution for criminal acts. One can, however, estimate the number of cases processed in a formal manner during the eighteenth century. Legally drawn up by alcaldes and other judicial officers and forwarded to the sala del crimen of the audiencia for confirmation and final disposition, such cases obviously represented only a fraction of the activity of judicial officers. In a like manner the acordada skimmed the top while local officials carried on the day to day enforcement of order without involving the institutional structure. One may assume, however, that the most serious crimes would be formally processed by the regular judical structure. By cautiously employing official statements and available statistics, it is possible to suggest the level of activity that concerned the authorities sufficiently to go to the expense of formal procedures.

According to viceregal statements, by 1759 the tribunal of the acordada already processed more cases than the sala del crimen and by the 1780s it supposedly accounted for four-fifths of all criminal cases in the viceroyalty.[31] The statistics maintained by the acordada reveal that between 1782 and 1789 the annual number of cases processed averaged 2,333.[32] If one accepts the figure as representing four-fifths of all criminal cases then the total number in the viceroyalty would only be 2,916. Compared to a population approaching the 5,800,000 figure noted by Baron von Humboldt in 1803, the number of cases processed does not seem impressive.[33] Even if one arbitrarily reduces the percentage of cases handled by the acordada to 50 percent or even one-third, the number of individuals involved in formal procedures in relation to the population would still be remarkably low. The minimal number processed supports the contention that the institutional judicial structure served as a reserve system called into action only when necessary to demonstrate the authority of the state. It also indicates that the local ad hoc method of enforcing order, with the legal system held in reserve, was a functional arrangement that kept criminal behavior at an acceptable level, although undoubtedly the low expectations of colonial authorities permitted greater latitude in behavior than was allowed among people of an equivalent social level in Spain. It may have been personally disturbing for the viceroys to preside over the multiracial society of New Spain; yet the relatively small percentage of cases officially processed indicates that criminal activity normally did not unduly tax the ability of the government to contain it within set limits.

The extent that informal methods predominated had the effect of distorting the percentages of cases processed in the various racial categories in relation to the overall population (see appendix). For example, while those of European origin made up approximately 18 percent of the population they contributed 28 percent of the criminal cases processed by the acordada and the sala del crimen. The Indian, representing 60 percent of the population, accounted for only 33 percent of the formal cases. The ratio of those classified as Spanish in relation to the overall population is almost three times that of the Indian. While other racial groups comprised 22 percent of the inhabitants they represented 39 percent of the cases: over three times the Indian ratio. The figures, rather than indicating a remarkable Indian attachment to law and order, emphasized the degree informal methods were employed. The urban-dwelling European or mestizo was more likely to be formally punished than the Indian.[34]

In spite of the relative ease of controlling deviant behavior, the marginal existence of the vast majority of the population created uncertainty and tension which affected the attitude of the government. As colonial authorities were aware, order could rapidly deteriorate, sparked perhaps by severe food shortages. Such a realization may partially explain the viceroy's attachment to the acordada, the very core of the formal judicial structure, which provided a reliable and effective defense in case of need, and in normal times served to represent viceregal order throughout New Spain.[35] Under the circumstances, the respect the acordada inspired may have been more important than the actual number of malefactors that passed through its prisons.

4 ORGANIZATION AND STRUCTURE

For much of the first two centuries of Spanish rule, the crown relied on local officials to maintain an acceptable degree of order without going to the expense and effort of involving the institutional system. The sala del crimen of the audiencia did not review, approve, or modify sentences imposed by lower officials as originally intended, although it did function as a primary enforcement agency in the capital and other areas. With the evolution of a more complex society composed of many different races and mixtures and engaged in varied economic activities whose impact went beyond limited regions, local justice could no longer adequately contain antisocial behavior. It became necessary to force the institutional structure to perform its intended functions, both to contain criminal activity that could not be dealt with on a local level and to impress on the population that the viceregal government possessed the legitimate authority as well as the ultimate power to enforce order.[1]

While the colonial government did not intend to dispense with the local ad hoc system that had functioned during the preceding centuries, it recognized the need for a reserve system. By the eighteenth century reality had to be faced no matter how reluctantly; hence, the sala del crimen resumed its legitimate functions at the pinnacle of the judicial process. At the same time, the tribunal of the acordada received the extremely important task of demonstrating that the viceregal government possessed the ability to contain the disorders that seemingly verged on overwhelming constituted authority. The tribunal's organization evolved throughout the eighteenth century and developed into the most important component of the viceregal judicial and enforcement system.

The acordada, in keeping with the objectives behind its formation, exercised unlimited territorial jurisdiction encompassing not only New Spain but the dependent kingdoms of New Galicia, New Vizcaya, and New León. No other tribunal in the viceroyalty possessed such responsibilities. The only area excepted was the Marquesado del Valle, where the crown conceded the right to administer justice to Cortés and his descendants. This exception lasted until 1785, when Madrid extended the acordada's jurisdiction to the marquesado.[2] Only the viceroy had the same jurisdiction. His authority, however, often proved difficult to maintain in the face of a large viceregal administration, two audiencias, and various provincial governors. The acordada, by contrast, was controlled from Mexico City by a judge independent of all territorial governors and judicial bodies, including the two audiencias of Mexico and Guadalajara. Unlike the viceroy, who could not remove royal appointees without the crown's permission, the judge extended and recalled commissions at his own convenience. The judge, directly subordinated to viceregal authority, answered only to the viceroy.

Moreover, regulations did not restrict acordada agents to one territorial jurisdiction, as in the case of ordinary justices, regardless of the fact the laws of the Indies emphasized the desirability of restricted territorial jurisdictions—limiting the exercise of authority to strictly defined areas in order to avoid unnecessary conflict between officials.[3] Any agent could operate outside his usual district, crossing the length and breadth of the viceroyalty if necessary, apprehending and formulating charges without hindrance from the ordinary justices in any jurisdiction. An acordada agent only had to present his commission to the alcalde mayor in his district of residence on appointment. This was not only a necessary formality but the document itself demanded the cooperation of the local authorities. An agent could request officials to supply aid and assistance under penalty of a fine of two thousand gold ducats for refusal.[4]

Under the first two judges, Miguel Velázquez de Lorea and his son José Velázquez de Lorea, the acordada's organization was informal. The remarkable energy of these two men and their obvious delight in personally leading their subordinates in pursuit of armed bandits made the tribunal a personal instrument of the Velázquezes. Its basic structure, however, would be set during their administration. This structure would later be regularized and strengthened by a set chain of command and definite controls centered in a core of salaried administrators.

Miguel Velázquez, organized the tribunal around a small group of paid administrators composed of a secretary and his clerk, a medical attendant, a chaplain, and a jailer.[5] Although the acordada jurisdiction was limited to rural areas until 1756, all these officials resided in Mexico City. This was in keeping with the well-known urban orientation of Spanish society as well as the organization's status as a viceregal creation. The tribunal's prison served as its central headquarters and as the residence of the judge. In the actual pursuit of malefactors, lieutenants and commissioner's who served without pay, assisted the judge.[6]

With the death of the first judge, the basic organizational structure had been set. José Velázquez de Lorea, who had previously served as one of his father's lieutenant's, made few changes as judge and captain. In 1747, however, the viceroy joined the separate office of the *guarda mayor de caminos* to that of the acordada.[7] At that time the colonial government placed the permanent guardhouses, which had been erected at notorious bandit lairs, under the tribunal's administration along with the twenty-one paid guards assigned to man the guardhouses and escort travelers through dangerous areas.[8] Subsequently, the Marqués de Cruillas, concerned about the methods employed by the acordada, ordered the appointment of an *assessor, defensor, procurador*, and secretaries to assist the judge in the administration of the tribunal. The viceroy charged these officials with the task of making the organization's procedures more formal and less summary. The king approved these structural changes in 1756, the same year that the second Velázquez died.[9]

With the death of José Velázquez, and in the absence of another member of the Velázquez family able to assume control, Jacinto Martínez de la Concha accepted the office of judge. Martínez was appalled at the lack of organization and the complete absence of any formal rules and regulations for the administration of the tribunal. He found the limited records of the acordada stuffed in boxes and closets in a state of neglect and disorder. More of an administrator than his two active predecessors, Martínez understood the need for an organized administration in the interest of both justice and efficiency. Nevertheless, the position of assessor and other assistants provided for by the Marqués de Cruillas to formalize procedures would be virtually eliminated during his tenure. The Marqués de Croix, convinced that the sale of convicts to provide funds for salaries had a detrimental effect on the administration of justice, prohibited the practice, leaving these officials without any compensation.[10] Consequently, an almost complete suspension of final sentencing of acordada prisoners resulted. The backlog of cases awaiting processing overcrowded both the ordinary jails and the prison of the tribunal. Martínez apparently refused to return to the informal practices of the Velázquez days to solve the problem. His lieutenant and successor, Francisco Antonio Aristimuño, solved the problem by appointing temporary assessors and defensors. In a period of six months Aristimuño sentenced 14 prisoners to death, condemned 433 to presidio terms, and released 180 as having served a sufficient sentence.[11]

It was apparent to the viceregal government that funds had to be found in order to keep the acordada from bogging down in a backlog of cases, as the cost of feeding and care of prisoners would eventually overwhelm the tribunal's limited financial resources and make impossible its continued activity. Turning to the pulque tax, from which revenue had increased because of the added pressure on violators of the prohibited liquor laws, the government levied an additional one grain of a real to support personnel necessary for the prompt handling and sentencing of prisoners.

In spite of Martínez's organizational problems, the most important change in the structure of the acordada occurred during his term. The problem of controlling prohibited liquors had long troubled the crown.[12] The only intoxicant legally permitted to be brewed was pulque.[13] Yet, the list of other intoxicants made locally was almost without end.[14] Cádiz shipowners complained that the carrying trade in wines and brandy, a major part of their business, suffered because of the competition with illegal liquors. In 1744 the crown, responding to these complaints, charged José Velázquez with the suppression of illegal intoxicants. Velázquez, already fully occupied in putting down banditry, proved unable to devote much effort to this secondary task. Recognizing that the acordada, as it existed under Velázquez, could not handle the effective suppression of prohibited liquors and also continue the primary task of clearing the viceroyalty of bandits, the crown sought another solution. The consulado of Cádiz proposed a four-real tax on each barrel of brandy entering New Spain, with the proceeds to pay the salary and costs of those within the acordada charged with the suppression of prohibited liquors. The crown, however, contented itself with renewing previous instructions to the justices to make a continued effort to enforce the laws.[15] Such legislative efforts, at best of minimal effectiveness, produced few results. The widespread use and manufacture of prohibited liquors could not be suppressed in such a fashion.

Pressure to create a separate body with full jurisdiction over prohibited liquors continued. Finally, the crown ordered the viceroy to choose a person suitable to head such an organization and indicate how it could be financed. Viceroy Revilla Gigedo proposed that a one-peso tax be placed on each barrel of brandy imported from Spain. With some reluctance Madrid gave Revilla Gigedo permission to set the tax at the required level. After some deliberation, the viceroy set the tax at four reals on each barrel of brandy and wine, and two reals on each barrel of vinegar entering Vera Cruz. On native-made legal intoxicants there would be a tax of two reals a barrel collected in Mexico City. The new tax, however, raised only 12,204 pesos, while the new tribunal required an estimated 16,000 pesos for its establishment. Revilla Gigedo suggested the difference be made up by a contribution from the merchants, who would obviously benefit from strict enforcement of the laws governing prohibited liquors. But the crown suggested that increased imports spurred by effective suppression would quickly make up the difference and ordered the viceroy to proceed with the establishment of the new body.[16]

Two problems delayed the establishment of the new tribunal: the lack of an able organizer to assume supervision, and the expense involved. In 1755 Revilla Gigedo ordered a comprehensive ordinance drawn up specifying the necessary officials and their responsibilities. The lack of funds, however, made it impossible to implement the ordinance.[17] Finally, in 1772 colonial officials conceded that the only body capable of implementing the prohibited liquor laws was the acordada.[18] Rather than merely adding the new duties to those already exercised by the tribunal, the authorities placed the *juzgado de bebidas prohibidas* under the judge as a separate jurisdiction.[19] Martínez was reluctant to take on the added responsibilities, citing the poor state of his health. As a compromise, the viceroy agreed to Martínez's request for an able lieutenant appointing Francisco Antonio Aristimuño to that post. On Martínez's death he would be advanced to the judgeship.

The importance of the addition of the juzgado de bebidas prohibidas lay in the financial support allocated to its operation. Inevitably, the judge commingled such funds with those of the acordada, and they became the financial backbone of the organization. Even after the legalization of native brandy and mescal, thus all but eliminating the work of the juzgado, tax support continued. Clearly to have abolished the juzgado and its supporting taxes would have been equivalent to eliminating the acordada.[20]

Prior to 1772 the tribunal had extremely limited funds at its disposal. The total financial support allotted the judge amounted to 14,000 pesos. Of this amount the consulado contributed 9,000 pesos, with the remaining 5,000 pesos coming from the city of Mexico in the sum of 3,000 pesos and 2,000 pesos from the viceroyal treasury. Technically, the government's 2,000 peso contribution went for the support of the office of guarda mayor de caminos. Out of this amount, the judge met the salaries of his paid staff, including the twenty-two highway guards, as well as providing for the sustenance of all prisoners unable to bear the cost of their own support. In addition, all extraordinary expenses involved in the apprehension of criminals, such as arms and horses for agents, were charged to the acordada. On top of this, the maintenance of the prison had to be met from the same pocket, leaving very little for the judge's own support. Martínez justly complained that this left "little more than nothing."[21]

With the placing of the juzgado de bebidas prohibidas under the judge's administration, the financial situation altered dramatically. The increased revenue at his disposal inevitably affected the organization of the tribunal. The acordada rapidly expanded its salaried staff supported by the revenue attached to the juzgado. By 1796 the number of individuals involved solely in the suppression of prohibited liquors totaled 27, with a total salary of 8,000 pesos a year.[22] Under the acordada's jurisdiction the number of paid agents rose from 30, including the 22 permanent highway guards, to a total of 83 with a total salary of 43,765 pesos, of which over half was supported by the prohibited liquor taxes imposed on legal li-

Organization and Structure

quors. The grand total of paid agents associated with the tribunal reached 110, with a combined salary of 51,765 pesos. In addition to fixed salary expenses, the acordada made an annual payment of 1,000 pesos a year to the women's prison. Major fluctuating costs, including medicines and the cost of feeding prisoners, ran from 7,000 to 9,000 pesos a year, of which about 2,000 pesos represented medical expenses and the remainder the cost of supporting the prisoners.[23] The tribunal's total annual expenditure now stood at approximately 60,000 pesos, a big jump from the pre-1772 figure of 14,000 pesos.

Income available to meet these expenses came from fixed contributions and fluctuating sources of which the prohibited liquor tax was the most important. The tribunal received 27,000 pesos annually drawn as follows: 2,000 pesos from the royal treasury, 3,000 pesos from the city of Mexico, 9,000 pesos from the consulado, and 13,000 pesos from the pulque revenue.[24] Of the fluctuating revenue, the most significant was that derived from prohibited liquor taxes. These taxes consisted, as mentioned previously, of a four-real tax on brandy and wine and a two-real tax on vinegar and legal native intoxicants entering the Mexico City market. The revenue collected from this source amounted to 30,000 pesos in 1799. By 1806 such revenue had risen to approximately 40,000 pesos.[25] In addition, several minor fluctuating sources of income contributed small amounts. Endowment by the pious provided approximately 3,000 pesos annually, and fines and condemnations contributed a relatively insignificant amount. Excess income, if any, was invested at the current interest rates and provided an occasional minor source of funds.[26] Generally the combined fixed and fluctuating income averaged from 60,000 to 70,000 pesos annually, just covering the expenses of the acordada. Occasionally, the tribunal had a modest 5,000 to 8,000 peso surplus and sometimes a deficit of the same amount. This income, however, permitted the tribunal to meet the demand for a more formal and regular administration of this important body.

Obviously, the funds of the acordada were not excessive nor did its support constitute a drain on the finances of the viceroyalty. The tribunal operated at far below the cost of any equivalent organization. Ninety-five percent of its agents served as unpaid volunteers operating at little or no expense to the viceregal government. Viceroy Revilla Gigedo observed that because of the acordada's low operating expense, its jurisdiction had been extended to cover a large number of offenses.[27] If the government had been forced to maintain the tribunal's volunteer force on a paid basis, it would have cost a minimum of 300,000 pesos annually.[28] The actual annual expense of 60,000 to 70,000 pesos may be compared to 133,038 pesos listed by Joaquín Maniau as salary expense of those charged with the regular administration of justice, excluding the cost of maintaining prisons and apprehending delinquents.[29] Maniau included under the heading of judicial salaries that of viceroy, the audiencia of Mexico and Guadalajara, the dependents of both audiencias, and the legal aides of the intendants. If the viceregal government had been forced to maintain a salaried acordada, the cost would have added a considerable burden to the viceregal treasury.

The judge, still in overall control of the acordada was now assisted on a regular basis by several officials with defined functions, and he could not get rid of them when he felt it convenient or expedient. Two assessors, ranked as first and second, a defensor, and two procuradores formed the judge's staff. Several general secretaries, also ranked as first and second, a secretary assigned solely to matters pertaining to the jurisdiction of prohibited liquors, and four clerks, one who dealt solely with cases involving the jurisdiction of prohibited liquors, assisted these top officials. To overcome past laxness in record-keeping, an official archivist received and filed the tribunal's records.

The two assessors alternately accompanied the judge when he left the city on official business to assure adherence to proper and formal procedures. They assumed jurisdiction over all cases temporarily suspended so that additional information and evidence could be gathered and it became their responsibility to see that the case was resumed as soon as possible. The regulation directed the defensor to defend the prisoners, a duty defined as seeing that justice was done, but without making any "frivolous pretexts."[30] The defensor served less to defend the prisoner than to check on the procedures used by the judge or assessors in processing and sentencing them. The defensor and the two assessors were empowered to receive the confessions of the prisoners.

The two procuradores assisted the defensor in monitoring the application of justice, making certain that all necessary papers followed the proper form. In addition, the regulations charged them with assisting and instructing the defensor in interviewing prisoners, as the occasion warranted. The procuradores also met with the two assessors and the defensor twice a week to assist in any clarification of matters under discussion.

The secretaries kept the records up-to-date, and on final sentencing of the prisoners deposited the records in the archive of the tribunal. They received also the processes remitted by agents outside the immediate area of Mexico City and held them in order, pending the arrival of the prisoners.

The assessors, defensors, procuradores, and secretaries served as administrators whose duties, so carefully prescribed, made the administration of the acordada more formal. The appointment of such a group of officials, through whom a process filtered until it reached the stage of sentencing, acted as a block to the arbitrary application of justice by the judge. With the exception of the assessors, these administrators were not involved except indirectly in the apprehension of criminals.

In the financial operation of the tribunal after 1772 the judge gradually lost direct control. The increased funds at his disposal necessitated some supervision by the viceregal administration. When the judge had only 14,000 pesos at his disposal, financial mismanagement merited little concern. Any records the judge kept of expenditures served only for his own convenience. With the additional funds placed at his disposal, however, formal control over expenditures became inevitable. A royal order in 1785 created within the acordada a separate accounting section, and in 1788 the viceregal government promulgated detailed instructions covering financial operations. These instructions provided for the adoption of standard fiscal procedures.

The accounting office and the judge assumed joint responsibility for the administration of the funds of the tribunal. Neither the judge nor the four officials of the accounting section—treasurer, accountant, and two secretaries—could operate without the consent and knowledge of the other. A strong box with three separate locks, with the keys distributed among the judge, the treasurer, and the accountant, held the current funds of the tribunal. One individual alone could not possess all the keys. In the event of the judge's absence, he passed his key to a lieutenant. In the absence of the treasurer or the accountant, the judge could take temporary possession of the absent members' keys, but could only open the strong box in the presence of one of the two secretaries standing in for the missing key holder. The treasurer and accountant maintained two separate sets of books, and in addition submitted a detailed monthly acounting to the viceroy, as well as providing a yearly audit and general inventory of the organization's assets. The treasurer and the accountant assumed joint responsibility for the submission of these reports, which underwent further audit by another accountant appointed by the viceroy to conduct a year-end review of finances. These procedures proved successful, and the charge of financial malfeasance was never raised even by the enemies of the tribunal. As an additional safeguard, the regulations required that both the treasurer and the accountant be bonded, the treasurer in the amount of 6,000 pesos guaranteed by three approved individuals, and the accountant in the amount of 2,000 pesos guaranteed by one approved individual.[31]

Apart from their own separate fiscal responsibilities, the judge, treasurer, and accountant shared a number of general obligations designed to eliminate any possible fraud by subordinates. To keep jailers from substituting or reducing the rations of the prisoners for their own profit, the regulation specified the exact amount and quality of rations. These officials bore the responsibility of taking an accurate daily count of the prisoners and assuring that the number of rations drawn matched the list of prisoners. The judge posted regulations regarding rations in several places within the prison so that the prisoners themselves could complain of any contravention. In the instance of any willful violation of these regulations, both the jailer and the actual dispenser of the rations received punishment in the form of a public flogging in full view of the prisoners. As a spot check, the judge, treasurer, or accountant occasionally dispensed the rations themselves. The rules prohibited the consumption of this food by nonprisoners and to avoid a conflict of interest, the rules also forbade the three officials or any intermediary to own or operate a store that supplied articles consumed by the prisoners.

The judge, treasurer, and accountant were jointly responsible for proper disbursement of the payroll, maintaining a separate record for each individual. The employee signed each time he received his salary. The law required all salaried dependents of the acordada, within a five-league radius of Mexico City, to collect their salary in person during the first eight days of the month. Agents outside of the five-league limit could delegate another person to receive their salary on their signed receipt. No alteration in the amount specified for each employee could be made without the approval of the viceroy.

In an effort to control fluctuating costs, the regulation directed the treasurer to stockpile food and fuel, buying the necessary cereals at harvest time and wood and charcoal at times of favorable prices.[32] Thus, the accounting section of the acordada removed most of the day-to-day financial responsibilities from the shoulders of the judge, making possible the smooth financing of operations in his absence. The judge, however, still shared sufficient responsibilities with the accounting section enabling him to keep informed of the tribunal's finances.

Only in the actual performance of the primary functions of the acordada did the judge's responsibilities remain untouched. Neither the viceroy nor the crown desired to inhibit the apprehension of malefactors. The colonial government recognized the advantages of the acordada both from the standpoint of civil order and its extremely reasonable cost. Consequently, the viceroy exercised great care, attempting to secure the best possible individual to fill the position of judge.

The father and son administration of the tribunal set a high standard for zeal and activity, if not formal justice. José Velázquez had demonstrated his competence to succeed his father, having served with distinction as a lieutenant. On the death of the younger Velázquez, however, his successor was not as clearly indicated. The Velázquez family theoretically held the office of judge on a proprietary basis, therefore, technically, the office should have remained in the family. The crown itself would have preferred to appoint another member of the family to the judgeship, having come to associate the magic name of Velázquez with civil order in the viceroyalty. José Velázquez's heir, Miguel, then only fourteen, could not assume such responsibilities, and an older brother lived in the Philippines.[33]

Although pressured to appoint the young Velázquez to the position, many, including the viceroy, considered the office of the judge too important to be entrusted to such an inexperienced candidate, even if he bore the name of Velázquez. With regret the crown chose Jacinto Martínez de la Concha.[34] Martínez had experience and an excellent record both as an alcalde mayor and a lieutenant of José Velázquez. Although Martínez at first declined the honor, the crown refused to accept his excuses. Madrid instructed Martínez to give the Velázquez heir some commission in the acordada in keeping with his age, and ordered that if the office of the judge fell vacant he be advanced to the position if his years permitted.

Martínez himself indicated his choice of a successor when he insisted on obtaining the services of Francisco Antonio Aristimuño as his lieutenant. Although Aristimuño had been groomed by Martínez, his appointment was not automatic. The viceroy carefully considered Aristimuño, then appointed him temporarily until he demonstrated his fitness to succeed Martínez as permanent judge of the acordada.[35]

The caution and obvious concern to appoint the most qualified individual clearly indicated the high value placed on the tribunal's services. The judgeship was not a post to be filled lightly, nor did favoritism play a significant part in the selection process. Throughout the eighteenth century the crown regarded it as an office so vital to the security of the viceroyalty that extreme care had to be exercised in filling the post with the most highly qualified individual available.[36] To be named temporary judge was not tantamount to obtaining the permanent position. Assessor Juan José Barberi served twice as interim judge. After the death of Aristimuño he held the position for two years, only to be replaced by a permanent appointment. Three years later he again served as judge for a year until the selection of another permanent judge.[37] The viceroy, with the crown's approval, selected the judge. Despite the fact that the audiencia had participated in the original establishment of the acordada, it did not exercise any control over appointments. The sala del crimen of the audiencia attempted several times to claim some voice in the decision but each time would be severely rebuked for its efforts. Although Madrid became increasingly concerned with entrusting too much power to colonial Americans in the latter part of the century, this does not appear to have been a consideration

Organization and Structure 65

in the selection process. The fact that the organization functioned under the direct authority of the viceroy, with few exceptions a peninsular Spaniard, may well account for the absence of imperial distrust.

Once appointed, the judge had full authority to select lieutenants and commissioners in any part of New Spain and its dependent kingdoms. Such appointments did not require the approval of the viceroy. Each commission united all the delegated powers and responsibilities of the tribunal of the acordada and juzgado de bebidas prohibidas in the same individual. No separate commissions were issued solely for the acordada or for any of the other jurisdictions placed under command of the judge.[38]

The difference between a lieutenant and a commissioner was more a matter of social position than a chain of command, although one or more commissioners usually assisted a lieutenant. The same duties and responsibilities were vested in each office, in fact both lieutenants and commissioners possessed identical printed commissions. The judge merely noted in the appropriate space the rank of the agent. A lieutenant, often either a hacienda owner or other respected resident of the district, usually a merchant, combined his personal influence with the wide jurisdiction of the tribunal of the acordada. For example, in San Juan del Río four lieutenants, six commissioners, and a horseman represented the acordada. All four of the lieutenants owned haciendas. Three of the *hacendados* actually resided on their property while the fourth lived in the town. Of the commissioners, four were connected with haciendas in some lesser capacity and the remaining two were town residents.[39]

The judge endeavored to choose from among European inhabitants whenever possible. In the most important cities this presented no difficulty, but in outlying areas the acordada often appointed lieutenants of mixed ancestry.[40] The desire for social prestige did not motivate people to seek a commission in the acordada. A commission was not an honor bestowed on worthy individuals by the king nor even the viceroy, but strictly a working commission accepted by the agents in the interest of protecting their own life and property. After the restoration of order, they frequently resigned their commissions. Rather than prestige, they sought the right to impose order. An acordada commission legalized summary methods and permitted them to establish order without the necessity of going through the local judicial authorities.

The more populated and important centers usually required at least one lieutenant in addition to the numerous unpaid lieutenants. By 1776 Puebla, Querétaro, Córdova, and Guadalajara each had one lieutenant considered important enough to be on a salaried basis.[41] It was impossible for the judge in Mexico City to know personally each candidate for a lieutenancy, In order to secure suitable individuals, the judge inquired among the responsible inhabitants of the area involved, such as local hacienda owners and principal merchants or officials of the towns. On the basis of these reports and recommendations, the judge made the appointment. With the introduction of the intendancy system in Mexico, the intendant, on request or on his own initiative, could suggest candidates, or express his opinion as to their suitability. Such an opinion did not have to be accepted; the judge, solely responsible for appointments, could extend or recall commissions at will.[42]

Commissioners were not chosen with as much care as lieutenants, although theoretically they exercised the same powers. The difference between the careful selection of lieutenants and the casual appointment of commissioners reflected the realities of the social structure in New Spain. A lieutenant possessed social and economic influence as well as the wide jurisdiction of the tribunal. As a result, he could wield considerable power in the district; hence, the individual's character became an extremely important consideration. An irresponsible lieutenant could severely disrupt society. A commissioner, however, did not have an influential social position and therefore could be controlled by "responsible individuals." Often a lieutenant suggested likely candidates for a commissioner's post, or local landholders or merchants would suggest appointments if they felt the need for a representative of the acordada in their area. Such requests almost automatically led to an appointment.[43] Commissioners were generally mestizos, often foremen on one of the local haciendas, who had been suggested by their employer. To these casual appointments may be traced many of the abuses that made the acordada notorious. As volunteers, all the unpaid appointees, whether lieutenants or commissioners, could resign their commissions at any time. They did not have an obligation to retain their posts until granted permission to retire as normally required.

No preconceived plan, other than the necessity of having a representative or representatives in heavily populated cities and areas, governed the distribution of lieutenants and commissioners. Based on need, the judge extended commissions without any thought to an even distribution throughout the organization's vast jurisdiction. As would be expected, the largest concentration of agents occurred in the more heavily populated areas of New Spain, especially in and around the viceregal capital. In Mexico City three lieutenants and seventeen commissioners, all on a salaried basis, represented the tribunal. In nearby Toluca the acordada had ninety-two unpaid volunteers; in Texcoco, forty-one; Cuernavaca, twenty-one; Tacuba, eighteen; and Tula, twelve. Puebla had seventy-six agents, including a paid lieutenant, while Guanajuato had fifty-nine. Port cities had a relatively small number of dependents, with only five in Acapulco and fifteen in Vera Cruz.[44] Outside the kingdoms of New Spain and New Galicia, the acordada was barely represented nor was the need pressing. The kingdom of New León had only one lieutenant, while New Vizcaya had two.

The freedom of the judge to appoint agents was one of the principal reasons for the success of the tribunal. Because the majority of the agents volunteered their services, the only consideration for appointment was the need for and the availability of suitable volunteers. In areas where the need existed, local interests could be counted on to supply the necessary personnel. Since the viceregal government did not place any restrictions on the number of unpaid dependents in any given area, trouble spots could be inundated with appointees.

As has been noted, the majority of unpaid volunteers served the rural areas of New Spain. This reflected the general insecurity of life and property outside the major cities. The paid agents were always stationed in the urban centers. The judge recognized that major cities required the full-time services of at least a few salaried agents. The number of acordada dependents constantly varied. After the addition of the juzgado de bebidas prohibidas to the responsibilities of the judge, the number of agents naturally increased, and by the end of the eighteenth century stabilized between 2,000 and 2,500 agents.[45]

As pointed out previously, the tribunal underwent several important changes after its inception in 1722. By the end of the century the informal organization of the Velázquez family had been replaced by a well-defined organizational structure. The tax revenue that accompanied the addition of the juzgado de bebidas prohibidas in 1772 enabled the acordada to expand and adopt a standard administrative organization. The judge, however, while relieved of many administrative and fiscal responsibilities, still bore the direct responsibility for the apprehension and punishment of delinquents.

5 ADMINISTRATION OF JUSTICE

If the acordada's territorial jurisdiction appeared to be simply and clearly defined, the same could not be said of its judicial authority. The tribunal's jurisdiction developed from the incorporation of theoretically existing bodies, each with its own special functions. To the acordada proper, which in turn grew out of the hermandad with its responsibilities, were added in succession the guarda mayor de caminos and the juzgado de bebidas prohibidas. From time to time the viceregal government added special duties to these major jurisdictions.[1] Instead of being incorporated into one title and jurisdiction, each of these offices, and its title, was maintained separately. Thus, the judge of the acordada concurrently held the titles of alcalde provincial de la santa hermandad, guarda mayor de caminos, and judge of the juzgado de bebidas prohibidas. These commissions, which had been extended by the judge, appointed agents as members of the hermandad, the tribunal of the acordada, and the juzgado de bebidas prohibidas, thus preserving the distinctions between jurisdictions.

The judge based the right to apprehend and charge a suspect on one of the separate jurisdictions under his command.[2] By virtue of the office of alcalde provincial of the santa hermandad, the acordada and its agents exercised authority over the crimes of robbery, physical violence, illegal seizure of property or women, arson, and the maintenance of private prisons, but only in villages or rural districts. If a suspect fled the city into a rural area, he could also legally be apprehended by the hermandad.[3] In the case of robbery, physical violence, or arson, the suspect could be apprehended within the city, if the crime had been perpetrated in an area that fell under the hermandad's responsibility. Banditry fell within the authority of the hermandad or the guarda mayor de caminos. If the permanent road guards seized the bandit, the jurisdiction of the guarda mayor de caminos applied while other agents of the acordada proceeded against bandits under the hermandad's powers.

The establishment of the acordada did not change the special jurisdiction of the santa hermandad except for one extremely significant modification. The hermandad was removed from judicial subordination to the sala del crimen of the audiencia. This exempted the tribunal from the obligation to report its sentences to the sala. The sentences of the acordada, exercising the jurisdiction of the hermandad, became final and without appeal to the sala del crimen. A further change occurred in 1756 when the viceroy ordered the judge to make day and night rounds within Mexico City with full authority over homicide, violence, and robbery. Subsequently, the tribunal received permission to operate in all populated areas on the same basis as in Mexico City.[4] The extension of the acordada's power to include population centers constituted an important change in focus.

While jurisdiction vested in the acordada itself only consisted of the tribunal's general exemption of its sentences from review by the sala, subsequently its authority would be broadened to include other responsibilities. The cumbersome authority united in the person of the judge in his many different capacities reflected the crown's reluctance to abolish offices as they became outdated.

The addition of the separate jurisdiction of the juzgado de bebidas completed the major duties exercised by the acordada. The judge received authority to apprehend and sentence all persons fabricating, consuming, or transporting illegal liquors, without regard to their race or social position. Nor could violators claim the protection of special fueros or jurisdictions, including military privileges.[5]

Under this system the judge of the acordada could move against almost all criminal offenses without regard to any territorial restrictions and freed from the embarrassment of having his sentence appealed to the sala del crimen. Even the Indians, who had previously enjoyed the privilege of being sentenced by local authorities in hermandad cases, fell under the tribunal's jurisdiction.[6]

The traditional haven of the church provided the only sanctuary from the tribunal's agents and even that proved more illusory than real. Certain classes of criminals were held to be ineligible to claim such protection, including highway robbers, notorious public thieves, persons guilty of treason, and murderers or those responsible for loss of part of a victim's body. In other cases agents removed suspects from churches if it could be done without interference from ecclesiastical authorities. When this was not possible, a statement could be taken with the permission of these churchmen.[7]

Under its first judge, Miguel Velázquez, the acordada administered the law with more emphasis on order than justice. The judge sentenced and executed offenders of hermandad crimes on the spot, but pressure to modify such an arbitrary application of justice quickly mounted. In 1724, acting on well-founded complaints of the sala del crimen in Mexico City that the acordada executed its sentences with little regard for justice or the laws, the crown attempted to correct the situation. A royal order instructed Miguel Velázquez henceforth to use the services of an assessor before and during sentencing to assure the proper substantiation of charges. The order, however, did not provide for any review of cases nor did it provide for appeals. It is difficult to imagine that it tempered the arbitrary justice administered by the tribunal. Velázquez's son José continued to employ the methods he had learned as his father's lieutenant. Despite instructions, no assessor was apparently used in the formulation and sentencing of prisoners.[8]

The pleas for a more tempered justice began to take effect only with the term of Jacinto Martínez de la Concha, who succeeded the second Velázquez. The sala del crimen in Mexico City, resentful of the acordada's freedom of action, generated much of the pressure. During the term of the first judge the sala's agitation resulted in the already noted royal order in 1724. Martínez himself felt the necessity of a more formal application of justice and instituted the practice of sentencing prisoners in the presence of an assessor and a secretary who discussed the case with the judge and signed the sentence. Responding to the demands for formal justice, Martínez began to evolve standard procedures and practices. In 1775 most of his procedures would be incorporated into a comprehensive document which detailed an agent's obligations and the companion regulations of 1776 which contained specific instruction concerning procedures.

Martínez directed that prisoners entering prison be carefully searched, and then they were to be placed in isolation until a statement could be taken. If a case involved two or more prisoners, they were separated to avoid the possibility of conspiracy to give false testimony. The regulation did not permit contact wih people outside the prison, either in writing or in person. In addition officials could only communicate with prisoners in an official capacity. Martínez even went so far as to employ guards unfamiliar with the Indian language and without any social or family ties with local inhabitants. Once the doors closed behind a prisoner, contact with the outside world ceased until approval of his sentence and its execution.

With the introduction of the *reglamento*, in a large measure the work of Martínez's lieutenant and successor Francisco Aristimuño, these simple procedures became institutionalized. In addition the regulations introduced safeguards designed to protect the accused from arbitrary practices. The viceregal government deemed the protection of the individual in acordada cases doubly important because of its exemption from the normal appellate authority of the sala del crimen. Thus, the reglamento represented a determined effort to bring the acordada's procedures more in line with acceptable standards of justice in the viceroyalty without, at the same time, risking its effectiveness by making its sentences subject to authority of the sala.[9]

The reglamento marked a radical departure from the judical philosophy of earlier acordada judges. A formal procedure had to be followed in the formulation of charges thereby avoiding ill-considered and overly hasty action. As a first step, an agent secured the assistance of the local notary, or in his absence a person of hidalgo standing, to assist in drawing up the charge, duly noting the circumstances of the crime as well as who reported it. Both the acordada agent and the notary then signed the charges before proceeding to apprehend the suspect although, if the accused attempted to escape, he could legally be detained first and the papers drawn up in the prescribed form later. No charges could be formulated against a minor under ten and a half years of age, or against a mentally deranged person. In event of a crime being perpetuated by such a person, the individual responsible for his conduct could be held, as could an accomplice acting with him.

After arrest, the offender was placed in complete isolation. If the local jail appeared insecure, or so small as to make it impossible to maintain the prisoner in isolation, he could be held in the agent's dwelling until a statement could be taken and his property impounded. Such a step limited the possibilities of the prisoner instructing his relatives or friends to dispose of his property or to arrange for alibis. It was also unquestionably of great psychological value in that it denied the prisoner any moral support or counsel from fellow prisoners or his family. With the suspect safely in custody, the acordada agent proceeded to take the sworn statement of the prisoner and the witnesses. Regulations did not permit the use of physical or mental coercion to obtain information.[10] If a crime involved more than one suspect, the agent compared their separate declarations and disposed of any serious differences by bringing the parties together to defend or modify their statements. Interpreters had to be present if the accused party spoke an Indian language. Mentally deranged persons, persons of ill repute, minors under twenty, known or declared enemies of the accused, as well as members of the family of the accused offender were prohibited from giving testimony. Each witness had to specify exactly how he came by the knowledge of the crime. The procedures attempted to eliminate hearsay evidence by narrowing down the testimony to the primary witnesses.

The regulation additionally required each agent to make his own investigation at the scene of the crime. In the case of a homicide, the officer personally inspected the corpse and certified that he had done so, noting the exact position of the body, the number and location of wounds or bruises, and the probable instrument employed. Then, in order to ascertain the cause of death, a surgeon, or in the absence of a surgeon the local barber or a person recognized as skilled in such matters, examined the body. The surgeon or his substitute signed a sworn certification that death had resulted from such wounds or blows. This procedure was also to be followed in cases of physical injury, even if the injured party appeared to be in no danger of dying from his wounds. In cases of rape the agent requested an examination by one or two matrons as well as by a surgeon before making any attempt to apprehend the suspect. The investigating officer also took all other testimony, although it was recognized that none might be available. Procedure required a face to face confrontation between the victim and the accused while charges were read.

In cases of robbery, arson, or the maintenance of private prisons, the regulation required the investigating agent to take equal care, personally inspecting and noting the circumstances and methods employed as well as taking the necessary sworn testimony.[12] If a prisoner died before sentencing, the case had to be carried to its conclusion in order to legalize the disposition of property or to indemnify the injured party. Improperly formulated cases were considered defective and were returned to the responsible agent for completion of the necessary procedures. A defective case did not free the prisoner; it simply prolonged his imprisonment before sentencing.

The regulations of 1776 emphasized considered examination rather than hasty, arbitrary action stemming from lack of prior substantiation of the charges. Yet, for every procedure noted there were exceptions that undermined the rule. A person could still be apprehended before the drawing-up of charges, using the pretext that he might escape. The notary could be replaced by a person of hidalgo rank, a status enjoyed by most people of any degree of wealth. A surgeon could likewise be replaced by a person of recognized medical knowledge. An agent had only to certify that the preferred procedure could not be employed.

In reality the regulations of 1776 proved too sophisticated for an organization such as the acordada. The volunteer status of the majority of the tribunal's agents worked against professionalism and the consequent refinement of police methods. The educational background of many of the commissioners of the acordada did not prepare them to understand and accept theory. In addition the constant turnover of such a volunteer force made it impossible to educate the agents to use such sophisticated procedures effectively. The fact that many hacendados or other influential inhabitants held a lieutenancy, and commissioners were frequently the employees of such powerful people, made it difficult to enforce strict compliance with the regulations. Their economic and social position, or that of their employer, combined with the acordada's powers made it easy to arrange things as they preferred. The audiencia rightfully observed that the freedom enjoyed by acordada agents from the interference of local judicial authorities made the agents indifferent to normal procedures, and in many cases the barest suspicion provided sufficient reason for them to force a confession. It is not difficult to imagine the ease with which they collected evidence in an area they so dominated. The vested interest of the local hacendados and merchants in the peace and security of their districts, together with the disdain held by the upper social and economic class for the lower classes, did not lead to an overconcern for justice. Order interested them above all else. They themselves were protected from arbitrary justice by their social and economic power. It is not surprising, therefore, that the protection of the accused as outlined in the reglamento of 1776 tended to be overlooked.

The absence of any time limit for the substantiation of charges meant that a prisoner could remain indefinitely in custody without being sentenced. Although intended to protect the accused from unfounded charges, the regulation often resulted in prolonged confinement for the suspect and he virtually rotted in prison. On the pretext of holding prisoners incommunicado, a number of agents actually operated their own private prisons. The dispatching of prisoners to Mexico City for sentencing, while protecting them from the arbitrary whims of the local agents, cut them off entirely from those who could testify in their defense. Denied outside contacts and exempt from the weekly inspections in regular prisons, the prisoner could not influence the progress of his case. The charge leveled by the audiencia in Mexico City that the acordada had become a tomb of the living did in fact have some substance.[13]

In crimes involving illegal liquors, the regulations indicated less concern with the protection of the accused than with practical suppression of such liquors. This reflected the crown's constant concern over the state of the royal treasury, as well as recognition that such a widespread and deeply rooted custom could not be effectively suppressed by anything less than arbitrary and ruthless enforcement. In 1775 Viceroy Revilla Gigedo authorized the regulations governing the administration and jurisdiction of the juzgado de bebidas prohibidas. When the acordada assumed the direction of this office, these regulations continued in effect. The administration of justice under the regulations of 1775 was direct and very practical. Like the other offices under the judge's jurisdiction, no appeals were permitted to the sala del crimen of the audiencia nor were prisoners apprehended under the authority of the juzgado to be included in the regular weekly visits to prisons. The judge or his dependents could operate in the capacity of agent of the juzgado de bebidas prohibidas in all parts of the viceroyalty. As agent of the juzgado, he was empowered to search without special permission, haciendas, ranchos, tapiches, sugar mills, warehouses, taverns, and pharmacies, as well as private dwellings, regardless of the official or social position of the owner.[14]

The concern of the government in the suppression of prohibited liquors was evident by the severe penalties imposed on offenders. An ordinance of 1735 set the minimum sentence at two hundred lashes and six years in the galleys, with permission to impose heavier penalties if justified by the circumstances. The following year a revision provided for confiscation and distribution of the confiscated property in equal parts to the agent, informer, and treasury. In addition Spaniards received six years of presidio confinement, while mestizos incurred the risk of a six-year term in workhouses and two hundred lashes. In 1742 a further modification provided either a four-year presidio term and a fine, or a straight six years for Spaniards. Indian chiefs and lesser officials incurred a four-year presidio term, while ordinary Indians received corresponding sentences to workhouses.[15] In 1778 the necessity of raising troops led to the offenders being sentenced to military service.[16] The weekly inspection of jails did not encompass prisoners accused of crimes involving prohibited liquors, unless specifically authorized by the viceroy or the agent responsible for the prisoner's apprehension. Although the regulation did not permit appeals, the viceroy approved all sentences before execution.

The acordada was not the only organization responsible for the suppression of illegal beverages. Every judicial officer in the viceroyalty theoretically bore responsibility. Local justices, however, under social pressure, did not insist on strict enforcement of the laws. It was charged, probably correctly, that many local officials had an interest in selling illegal liquors, or chose to ignore their use.[17] As established members of the community, they hesitated to disrupt society with active persecution of those following such a widespread custom. Unquestionably, the acordada, using the authority of the juzgado de bebidas prohibidas, became the principal means of controlling illegal liquors. Yet, even that tribunal provided only minimal control, generally confining its efforts to the vicinity of the capital.

In the Mexico City area the judge assigned twenty-two salaried agents exclusively to the task of suppressing prohibited liquors. Outside the immediate vicinity of the city, only a small number of salaried agents pursued offenders. Puebla had two agents and the cities of Querétaro, Córdova, and Guadalajara had only one agent each.[18] It should be remembered that agents of the acordada also carried commissions as agents of the juzgado de bebidas prohibidas. But, mainly concerned with the suppression of banditry and other crimes against life and property, they had little time to devote to suppression of illegal dealings in liquor. Recognition of this fact prompted the appointment of the salaried agents mentioned above. Over 50 percent of the arrests for violations of the prohibited liquor laws occurred in the vicinity of Mexico City. Nevertheless, the number of persons apprehended for crimes involving illegal liquors was never very great.

Martínez processed only 881 individual cases during an eleven-year period, of which only 177 warranted major sentences. The remainder received simple punishment, often a public flogging. Martínez's successor, Santa María, with characteristic zeal, processed 2,002 cases between 1782 and 1792, of which 691 involved major sentences. In the 28 year period from 1763 to 1792 the tribunal processed only 4,151 cases, an average of 149 a year, and this figure included those freed after simple punishment.[19] Santa María averaged a slightly more impressive 202 a year. The impossibility of any truly effective suppression of these liquors would eventually lead to the legalization of both mescal and cane brandy. Yet, the tribunal's efforts appeared to be successful, up to a limited point—at least the crown attributed the rising pulque revenues to the acordada's efforts to suppress prohibited liquors.

The treatment of prisoners once they reached the prison in Mexico City did not, in theory, differ from the treatment accorded those in any royal prison.[20] The difference lay in the rigid enforcement of the regulations and the fact that the tribunal deprived prisoners of contact with the outside world. In effect they seemed to disappear, a feature that made the acordada prison a place to be feared. Such a policy inevitably led to the circulation of the wildest type of rumors. Loose talk led to a surprise inspection of the prison by Viceroy Matías de Gálvez. The viceroy, pretending to be interested in inspecting the newly constructed headquarters of the dragoons, arrived unannounced at the gates. He then demanded the keys and proceeded to inspect the prison, including the hospital and the kitchen, noting the quality and quantity of the food. Not limiting himself to a mere physical inspection, the viceroy carefully interviewed a number of prisoners awaiting execution. Gálvez, visibly impressed with the efficiency of the operation and with the treatment of prisoners, commented that the prison of acordada was "not like they told me."[21]

The overwhelming majority of prisoners crowded into the acordada's jail were charged with hermandad offenses. The tribunal's energetic implementation of its hermandad authority far outstripped efforts to suppress illegal liquors. Under its most important jurisdiction, the acordada concentrated on crimes involving property, a concern that personally interested the organization's volunteer agents as well as the viceregal authorities. Theft of livestock and robbery, the two classifications of crimes most frequently processed by the acordada, comprised well over 50 percent of all cases, irrespective of race. A comparison of the tribunal's cases with those of the sala del crimen clearly demonstrates the tribunal's emphasis on property crimes. Theft of animals accounted for 28 percent of the Spaniards processed by the acordada and only 2 percent of the sala's cases, while robbery constituted 36 percent of the tribunal's cases as opposed to the sala's 14 percent. The exact reverse occurred with purely social offenses. Of Spaniards arrested by the acordada, only 4 percent were charged with homicide while the sala del crimen processed 34 percent for that crime. In the same manner the tribunal's vagrancy arrests accounted for a mere 3 percent as compared to 23 percent of the sala's cases. Comparative figures on all four of the major racial groups (see appendix) confirm the basic pattern, with some significant differences.

The incidences of homicide among the Indians provides one such departure from the overall pattern. Homicide supplied 11 percent of the acordada's Indian arrests but a staggering 85 percent of the sala's. It is interesting to note that the percentage differential between Spaniards and Indians arrested for homicide by both the acordada and the sala del crimen is almost identical—250 percent more Indians apprehended for that crime than Spaniards. This may offer some support for the sociological theory that the number and frequency of violent crimes is directly linked to the degree of self-respect of a particular group.

Another interesting departure from the general pattern is the insignificant number of Indians sentenced for vagrancy as compared with Spaniards. Apparently local judicial officers did not view Indian vagrancy as a serious enough problem to warrant referring cases to the sala, while the acordada, concentrating on property crimes, ignored social problems. Many Spaniards gravitated to urban centers such as the capital itself, and the authorities felt constrained to curb these vagrants, as indicated by the statistics. Possibly Indians did not react in any signficant number to adverse living conditions by becoming vagrants. Their low economic and social expectations, in marked contrast with those of Spaniards, normally could be fulfilled at a subsistence level. Temporary vagrancy to avoid tribute or other vexatious obligations may well have been truancy rather than the vagabondage that afflicted other racial groups.[22]

The small number of arrests for sexual offenses provides further proof of the acordada's reluctance to expend effort to curb deviant behavior. Enforcement of the laws regarding such crimes was left almost entirely to local officials. A significant number of cases went through formal channels with final sentencing pronounced by the sala del crimen, indicating that the authorities viewed rape, incest, and sodomy as serious offenses. The acordada, however, in keeping with its preoccupation with property crimes, ignored such purely social crimes. By the same token a relatively small number of property crimes filtered up to the sala from local officials, as compared with the number handled by the tribunal, suggesting that local justices either preferred to deal with them informally or left enforcement to the acordada.

Punishment varied in accordance with the crime and race of the offender. Generally, only the most heinous acts merited the death penalty. Notorious incidents of banditry or robbery with excessive violence often resulted in a public hanging; yet, a relatively small number actually received capital punishment. During Santa María's term as judge (1782–1808), only 246 individuals faced the gallows compared to 10,244 condemned to presidio terms and another 30,979 released after simple punishment. At the other end of the scale, petty criminals might be held several months in the tribunal's prison before being released without further punishment or sentenced to labor in the capital's public works.²³ Those who fell in between the two extremes usually received presidio sentences of one to ten years. Such criminals might also be sentenced to corresponding terms of service on board His Majesty's ships or in a military unit.

Indians, however, did not receive sentences involving military service and only occasionally were they sentenced to ship duty. In addition, the Indian, as well as the various mixed castes and even Spaniards, could be sold to private employers as convict labor. The price in 1717 of such workers ranged from 39 pesos a year to 182 pesos for ten.²⁴ The so-called *reos de collera*, however, were more prevalent in preceding centuries. Nevertheless, obraje sentences appear to have been imposed, although in reduced numbers, into the nineteenth century.²⁵

In the eighteenth century presidio confinement emerged as the most important formal punishment for all groups. Except for rare cases, Indians served their sentences in presidios within the area of the modern Mexican republic, usually in Vera Cruz. Occasionally, however, the tribunal dispatched hostile Indians, captured on the northern frontier during one of the constant Indian wars, to overseas presidios.²⁶ All other castes could be sentenced to confinement inside the kingdom of New Spain or overseas, as well as to naval and military service.²⁷ The controlling factor appears to have been labor needs of the various presidios to build or maintain fortifications and harbor improvements, although viceregal authorities urged that those sentenced to overseas locations be sent for a minimum of three years because of the transportation expense.²⁸ Of the three racial categories—Spaniards, mestizos, and mulattoes—subject to overseas sentences, 78 percent received such punishment. An overseas presidio sentence might also include a prohibition against the convict returning to New Spain without special permission after serving his term. On occasion the sentence required criminals born in Spain be returned to that country on completion of their confinement.

The offender's age and physical condition received due consideration when sentence was passed, as did the length of time spent in custody before conviction. Young men in good health stood a better chance of ship or military service, while the aged or ill would be sentenced with a recommendation that they be employed in some capacity in keeping with their condition, perhaps in the hospital or infirmary and occasionally service within the acordada prison itself. Indian caciques could expect the same punishment as ordinary Indians with only one concession to their superior status—exclusion from certain types of heavy labor. The authorities also frequently allowed the same privilege to individuals taken from church asylum, perhaps the result of an agreement between ecclesiastic authorities and the tribunal to be as merciful as possible.[29] Slaves received presidio terms on the same basis as freemen, but at the end of their sentence they remained in custody at their owner's expense until collected or returned. An owner might deed his slave to the crown so that on termination of the sentence the authorities could dispose of the individual as they chose.[30] The majority of acordada prisoners served their terms in the presidios of Havana or Vera Cruz. Significant numbers, however, also went to Acapulco, Piedras Negras, Pensacola, and, in rare instances, to the Philippines and other areas of the Spanish empire.

The length of presidio sentences did not vary according to an individual's racial classification. Those classified as Spaniards recevied roughly the same terms accorded the other groups. Yet, there is some indication that supplementary punishment in the form of a flogging was more often imposed on mestizos and mulattoes than on Spaniards and Indians. The evidence suggests that mestizos and mulattoes incurred twice the risk of such punishment than the other two major groups. Prior to 1786 indefinite sentences could be imposed. The fear of interminable confinement, however, often led to escape. By restricting sentences to a ten-year maximum and by requiring judicial agencies to indicate a fixed term it was hoped that presidio prisoners would not resort to desperate measures.[31] Sentences for ordinary homicide ran from one to a maximum of ten years, with an average term of approximately five and one-half years. Vagrancy merited from two to four years, often ship service rather than a presidio term. Theft of animals resulted in an average term of three and one-half years but could go up to the maximum of ten years. The average sentence for robbery tended to be slightly higher, falling between three and one-half to four years, also with a maximum of ten years.

Condemned prisoners had no appeal from acordada sentences but could petition the viceroy, seeking the king's mercy. A petition was not considered a legal appeal, merely a simple request for mercy. The crown expected the viceroy, as the king's representative, to demonstrate benevolence on occasion. Viceroy Gálvez provided an example of this attitude when he inadvertently passed the acordada's gallows just as sentence was to be executed. The condemned men immediately threw themselves on the king's mercy, and Gálvez felt obligated to commute their sentences. The crown approved his actions but ordered that in the future the viceroy be advised of the exact hour of executions so that he could avoid being forced to exhibit the royal benevolence.[32]

General pardons in celebration of important royal events such as coronations, marriages, and births, provided a more dependable source for clemency than a chance extension of royal favor. Although far from extensive, such pardons resulted in the release of a substantial number of prisoners. All judicial officers, including the judge of the acordada, submitted cases for consideration by the sala del crimen or a special provisional officer appointed specifically for that purpose.[33]

Certain crimes, such as lese-majesty, murder of a priest, blasphemy, sodomy, arson, dueling, robbery, counterfeiting, fraud, and resisting arrest, did not fall under the terms of the pardon. Those who had fled or escaped from custody could turn themselves in within a specified time limit to take advantage of the terms of the general pardon. Even fugitives apprehended within the expressed period qualified for consideration. The largest category included in the general pardon was acts of violence not attended by robbery. Individuals guilty of such crimes, or considered fugitives, had their sentences reviewed.

In addition to releasing prisoners, a general pardon eliminated many pending cases, providing the guilty party turned himself over to the authorities, and thus reduced the number of unresolved cases that threatened the public's belief in the inevitability of punishment and at the same time demonstrated the crown's power to alter criminal status. The important exception of cases involving robbery and fraud was made because these crimes affected private property. The crown's respect for property is clearly evident in the conditional release of debtors under the terms of a pardon. Released debtors had thirty days of freedom to reach some agreement with their creditors. Although debtors might be financially assisted by the "royal munificence" to satisfy their debts, the crown did not attempt to erase private obligations.[34]

The absence of regular appeals left the accused at the mercy of the tribunal. The acordada's judicial independence inevitably led to lax practices and miscarriages of justice. It was such a miscarriage that finally resulted in the installation of a review board in the last decade of the eighteenth century. In 1787 the acordada routinely processed, among others, two cases, one involving homicide and the other robbery with physical violence. Of the four men involved, two received capital sentences. The death sentences of the two prisoners would have passed unnoticed except for the concern of a priest who came into official contact with one of the condemned and considered the sentences to be unduly harsh.[35] The priest appealed to the viceroy for mitigation of the sentences on the grounds that the homicide had been committed under the influence of pulque, while hunger motivated the robbery— apparently a common occurrence in times of shortage. The viceroy, acting on the advice of his assessor, suspended the sentences. Meeting with the audiencia in consultative session, he reviewed the cases in question. Unavoidably, the acordada's overall administration of justice was subjected to a critical evaluation.[36]

The principal reforms advocated by the audiencia were not new. Most important, the oidores proposed to permit the right of appeal in acordada sentences, and recommended that the tribunal's prisoners be included in normal prison inspections. It was also suggested that outside the Mexico City area acordada agents be subordinated to the intendant, while its actual territorial jurisdiction be limited to Mexico City, Puebla, and Vera Cruz—the areas of greatest need.

In view of the number of cases handled by the tribunal, and to avoid overburdening the regular sala del crimen with appeals, the audiencia suggested that a separate sala for appeals of acordada sentences be established, with the same rights and remuneration as the regular sala del crimen.[37] This sala would also approve the appointments made by the judge, a step deemed necessary to control the number and quality of the tribunal agents. The proposed sala would also be responsible for making the regular prison inspections, advocated in the recommended reforms, and for releasing those found to be illegally imprisoned. Three annual general inspections of the acordada prison would be made by the audiencia, as was customary with regular prisons. These recommendations, if followed, would have subjected the tribunal to the same controls imposed on ordinary justices. Technically, the acordada would still not be subordinated to the sala del crimen, but in fact the proposed appeal board, with the same rights and remuneration, would have been an extension of the sala.

The inability of the acordada to consider mitigating circumstances, as exemplified by the two cases in question, emphasized the tribunal's preference for order over justice. Both individuals were guilty and the guilty had to be punished. Such a simplistic view of justice was a disturbing feature of the organization. Yet, at the same time, this intransigent attitude, in large measure, accounted for its success. Offenders could not expect the tribunal to show any mercy; thus, to bring the acordada's vengeance down on one's self was a fate to be avoided. The government would have preferred to have order with justice. Such a combination, however, could not be achieved through a volunteer force, and the crown was not prepared to bear the expense of a salaried police force. This dilemma accounted for the ambivalent attitude of the viceroys and the crown. The authorities realized that if the acordada's justice was to be tempered, some type of effective control would have to be established. Yet, any restrictions might hamper the tribunal's efficiency, with consequent ill effects on order.

The response of the crown, in the case of the men sentenced to death, attempted to meet the requirements of justice as well as order. A royal *cédula* of 19 September 1790 commuted the sentences of the two condemned individuals to long presidio terms. In addition the cédula provided for the setting up of the *junta de revisión* (junta of revisions) composed of one member of the sala del crimen, the assessor of the viceroyalty, and a lawyer to review all sentences involving capital punishment, torture, public flogging, or similar types of public shame, with power to approve or modify such sentences. In order not to cause excessive delay in carrying out the sentences of the acordada, such a review had to be made in fifteen days or less.[38] The crown's response fell far short of the reforms proposed by the audiencia. The junta, not being an appellate tribunal, functioned strictly as a review board and only in limited cases. Nor was the junta or the audiencia given permission to conduct regular prison inspections to insure legal confinement. The judge continued to make appointments on his own authority without any restrictions. The junta had to rely on the evidence presented by the acordada in each case reviewed, and hence could do little but check for obviously defective cases and limit excessive punishment.

In spite of the obvious weaknesses of the junta of revisions, it cannot be dismissed as of little consequence. It did force an immediate tightening-up of procedures, causing the acordada to operate more in the spirit of the regulations of 1776. The practice of drawing up abstracts of all cases, as provided for by law, had long been neglected by the assessors of the tribunal. Over the years the assessors depended more on their memory than appeared compatible with justice. An oral review of the principal facts had become the practice before sentencing. With the necessity of presenting the entire file to the junta of revisions, the question of abstracts became an issue. The junta rightfully noted that the memory could not be relied upon and questioned the legality of dispatching cases by oral review alone. More than a concern for justice motivated the junta. The absence of abstracts forced junta members to plow through piles of testimoy and form their own abstracts.[39] The acordada, in return, insisted that the formulation of abstracts constituted an unnecessary waste of time and if followed would cripple the dispatch of business. The crown finally resolved the matter in 1802 by ordering the judge to comply in all cases subject to junta review.

The review of sentences by the junta and the return of defective cases pressured the acordada to instruct its agents, many of whom must have been only dimly aware of the comprehensive regulations of 1776, in drawing up abstracts and tightening procedures. The number of defective cases returned by the junta caused Santa María to request permission to distribute five hundred free copies of the regulation, and another two thousand copies at the minimum cost of twenty reales each. The fact that José Barberi, who had himself twice provisionally held the office of judge of the acordada, served as a member of the junta of revisions made it impossible for the tribunal to bluff or conceal compromising practices.[40] Santa María keenly resented any restrictions placed on his authority and constantly demanded the suppression of the junta of revisions. He complained that the junta was too slow and charged that in delaying the execution of the sentence, it inflicted further punishment on the prisoner and, moreover, such delays impaired the efficiency of the acordada. Santa María's pleas for the suppression of the junta were not well received. The audiencia suggested that if the viceroy suppressed the junta, the acordada be subordinated to the judicial authority of the sala del crimen.[41]

The charges of inefficient and prejudicial delay leveled at the junta of revisions were well founded. The junta considered the fifteen-day limitation for reviewing cases unreasonable and, consequently, ignored it. The assessor of the viceroyalty, already fully occupied with his own duties, as was the sala del crimen member, left most of the task to Barberi, who could not handle it alone. The unrealistically small composition of the junta eventually forced the viceroy to name more provisional members to clear up the backlog. The crown initially approved the permanent addition of one of the provisional members. On further consideration, however, it decided that since no backlog existed, the addition was unnecessary. Yielding to complaints that the assessor of the viceroyalty, overburdened with his primary responsibilities, could not assume additional functions, the crown relieved him of all duties on the junta. A member of the sala del crimen replaced the assesor for a six-month term.[42] Every six months another member of the sala took a turn on the junta. Now composed of two members of the sala del crimen and a lawyer, the junta's composition differed little from that originally proposed by the audiencia, although it had none of the authority that the oidores had recommended. It was strictly a review board and not an appellate court.

While Santa María could hardly have been pleased by the addition of another member of the sala del crimen, the composition of the junta mattered little. The two members of the sala, because of the press of other business, could not devote full time to reviewing acordada cases. Inevitably, Barberi, as the only full-time member of the junta, carried the main responsibility. The crown, unwilling to financially support a sufficiently large number of members, even charged Barberi's salary against the funds of the acordada.

In addition to lacking sufficient personnel, the junta did not have a set work schedule, meeting at the convenience of the members. In spite of these weaknesses and the complaints of the judge, the junta did not adversely affect the efficiency of the tribunal. Santa María, an active judge, processed 42,671 prisoners during his twenty-six year tenure. In the three years following the organizing of the junta, the number of prisoners processed by Santa María did not reflect any restriction of his activities.[43]

The junta of revisions represented a significant concession to public pressure as well as to the concern of other judicial officials. The viceregal government, vitally concerned with the order and security of the viceroyalty, generally held whatever reservations they had concerning the tribunal's methods in check, but recognized the need to establish at least nominal control over the acordada's actitvities. To not have done so would have risked widespread resistance to the acordada and a consequent undermining of its effectiveness.[44] The junta served the purpose by instituting a measure of judicial review while the acordada's functions remained substantially unchanged.

6 ACORDADA AND ITS OPPONENTS

In theory the acordada's territorial and judicial jurisdiction made it the most powerful of all judicial bodies in the viceroyalty. Although the tribunal enjoyed wide authority, it did not supersede the other judicial bodies that remained and functioned along with the acordada. Two distinct systems discharged criminal justice in the viceroyalty: the traditional system with the sala del crimen at the top, and the acordada. Neither system had exclusive jurisdiction over criminal offenses. The acordada's legal authority, far from all-inclusive, rested on the incorporation of theoretically existing bodies, each with its own jurisdiction and previously more or less inactive. Through the years the responsibiltities of these agencies had been assumed by the ordinary justices. With the establishment of the tribunal, however these jurisdictions were in theory removed from the hands of the local judicial authorities, no simple task. Over a period of a century, the distinctions between jurisdictions had been ignored.

Legally the acordada had to define offenses placing them under one of the jurisdictions vested in the tribunal, before proceeding to process them. The open question of definition made it possible for both the acordada and other judicial officers to claim the right to proceed in almost any given case. Which crimes fell to the tribunal and which were reserved for other agencies proved a constant source of confusion and contention. In many cases, such as violations of the prohibited liquor regulations, all judicial authorities legally exercised authority, further complicating matters.

In addition to jurisdictional conflicts, institutional jealousy prompted other agencies to seize upon any pretext to obstruct the acordada's activity. Serious resistance came from the members of the sala del crimen of the audiencia, who, although deprived of any control over the tribunal, enjoyed a higher status as crown officials and did not hesitate to use their prestige against all opponents. In an attempt to bestow the same status on the judge of the acordada, the crown instituted the practice of conferring an honorary membership in the audiencia on every judge after José Velázquez—Martínez de la Concha being the first to receive this honor.[1] Such an honorary appointment had little effect on the relations between the acordada and the sala del crimen. The members of the sala, as crown officials, felt obliged to complain about anything that affected what they considered the welfare of the king's subjects.

Although they had originally concurred with the necessity of creating the acordada and freeing it from subordination to the sala, the judges quickly regretted their action. The sala del crimen assumed an unfavorable attitude toward the tribunal it helped create almost from its very establishment. Consistently, throughout the acordada's entire existence, the sala pressed for two main reforms that would have placed the organization under its supervision. The sala demanded that appeals be allowed and that the audiencia conduct routine prison inspections and release those prisoners found to be illegally detained. The desire for these two reforms underlay every dispute between the sala and the tribunal. Above all, the sala wanted to regain its position as the highest criminal court in the viceroyalty, a position it was unwilling to share with any agency. The audiencia also deeply resented the judge of the acordada's exemption from the *residencia* process, an official review of an individual's conduct in office to which all other judicial offiicers, including the viceroy himself, were subjected. With some justification, the oidores maintained that the judge was the most privileged magistrate in New Spain.[2]

In addition to the opposition of the sala del crimen in Mexico, the audiencia of Guadalajara also resisted the acordada's authority, seeming to resent the existence of a Mexico-based organization that it had no part in creating. These two bodies could rely on a steady stream of complaints against the acordada from local officials. The combined influence and actions of the tribunal's opponents never quite overwhelmed the organization but occasionally came close. In fact, if not in theory, these opponents constituted an effective counterbalance to the acordada's authority.

While regretting the necessity of such a body as the acordada, the viceroys generally backed it in its many disputes, often torn between a sense of justice and the priorities of internal order. The specter of internal disorder constantly forced the viceroys to place order before justice. It would be erroneous, however, to picture a weak acordada huddled under the viceroy's protective wing. When occasionally the viceroy changed the priorities, the tribunal could ably defend itself. The acordada made its point merely by permitting the inefficient sala del crimen and local authorities to bear the full burden of enforcement. In at least one case the judge of the acordada virtually blackmailed the viceroy into supporting the tribunal and on occasion the judge appealed to the crown over the viceroy's head. Only through the study of the acordada's conflicts with other judicial officials does an accurate picture of its place within the system emerge. The forces balanced against the acordada and the constant ebb and flow of their influence fixed the tribunal's place within the judicial framework of the viceroyalty.

The royal cédula approving the acordada's creation arrived in 1722. Less than a year later the sala del crimen opened its campaign, charging that the tribunal exercised powers denied even "ministros togados" and that Miguel Velázquez ignored proper procedures. The sala complained that the judge of the acordada denied the right of appeal and refused to allow the audiencia to inspect the tribunal's prisoners and, worst of all, the judge sentenced prisoners to presidios in the Philippines.[3] The crown responded by reaffirming Miguel Velázquez's authority, instructing him, however, to use the services of an assessor in the formation of charges and in the sentencing of prisoners. The assessor supposedly would advise the judge on the legal exercise of his authority. The crown expressed the hope that the use of such an official would eliminate further squabbles between the sala del crimen and the acordada.

The following year the sala again complained that Miguel Velázquez, disregarding the law on one pretext or another, failed to utilize the assessor's services. The crown, in response, reaffirmed its previous order, and in addition ordered the acordada to consult with the sala del crimen after execution of the sentences to determine if the case had been properly handled. This apparently would only be necessary in the event of a dispute between the two agencies. Velázquez appears to have ignored these instructions.

The judge countered the charges of the sala del crimen by constantly harping on the uncertain state of order in the viceroyalty and the sala's excessive caution in handling such disorders "even if it resulted in the ruin of these domains."[4]

During José Velázquez's tenure as judge the tribunal began to operate within Mexico City. Such an extension of the acordada's jurisdiction was illegal. It will be recalled that only in 1756, the same year José Velázquez died, was the jurisdiction of the acordada legally extended to the city. Velázquez did not pay too much attention to legalities, since the illegal operation of his organization within the city of Mexico had been encouraged by important persons there who had more faith in the tribunal's efficiency than in that of the sala. When a burglary attempt was made at the convent of San Francisco in 1753, the authorities immediately requested Velázquez and his men to conduct the investigation. The same year the viceroy availed himself of the services of the acordada to solve a robbery involving one of his servants. The servant had cunningly removed the keys from the viceroy while he slept and helped himself to the silverware, replacing the keys before the unsuspecting official awoke.[5] Velázquez, with customary efficiency, investigated the case and seized the guilty party.

The activities of the tribunal within the capital brought the acordada and the sala del crimen into a direct struggle over jurisdictions. In 1754 the state of disorder within Mexico City prompted the viceroy to support the extension into the city of the tribunal's jurisdiction. The subsequent formal request of the acordada for this extension shocked the sala out of its excessive caution. Taking note of the acordada's obvious success in controlling crime, the sala proposed to bestow the same freedom to apprehend and sentence on its dependents, without destroying its own position as the highest level of the judicial system. The sala suggested that the ordinary justices be relieved of the necessity of reporting their sentences to the sala del crimen. In case of an appeal, they were to execute the sentence first, then turn the entire file over to the sala for consideration. If such a request had been granted, there would have been little distinction between the acordada and other agencies. Madrid did not agree and, in fact, accused the sala del crimen of using normal disorders, common to all cities, as a pretext to extend illegal authority to its dependents. The crown reviewed the reason for the existence of the high court and noted that if it granted such a request the next logical step would be the extinction of the sala. The crown then proceeded to outline the sala's responsibilities and emphasized its opposition to any change.[6]

With the death of José Velázquez in 1756, the sala del crimen contested the right of the viceroy to name even a temporary replacement, alleging that since the king had invested the office of judge in the Velázquez family, only the crown could transfer such proprietary rights.[7] The viceroy ignored this specious argument as well as the subsequent attempts by the sala to have some part in the selection of a successor to Velázquez.

In 1756 the crown legally extended the jurisdiction of the acordada to include day and night patrol in Mexico City, in the same manner as the agents of the criminal court. This extension remained uncontested until 1771 when the sala alleged that a cédula of September 15 of that year, which had ordered the Marqués de Croix not to hinder it in the exercise of its duties, reaffirmed its authority. The court interpreted this to mean that they could resume exclusive police control in Mexico City and limit the acordada strictly to the jurisdiction of the hermandad. The viceroy acquiesced until the alarming increase in violence in Mexico City prompted him to disregard the sala and order the tribunal to resume its patrol.[8] Using the same cédula of 1771, the sala del crimen pressed the viceroy to permit appeals in cases handled by the acordada which were not under the jurisdiction of the hermandad. This would have made all cases resulting from the tribunal's patrols within Mexico City subject to the sala's approval. Viceroy Bucareli, however, who had observed the effects of barring the tribunal's patrols from the city, avoided further complications by referring the question to Spain and meanwhile ordered that no change be instituted.[9]

The cédula of September 19, 1771, continued to be used by the sala del crimen to harass the acordada and pressure the viceroy. In 1775 that court, chafing at Bucareli's lack of sympathy for its demands, complained to the king that the viceroy had despoiled it of its authority and amplified the powers of the acordada in violation of the cédula of September 19, 1771. The response of the crown must have been an unwelcome surprise. Instead of backing the sala, the crown declared that the cédula of 1771 did not abridge in any way the authority of the acordada or restrict its jurisdiction and, to emphasize the point, annulled the cédula in each instance where it conflicted with the previous cédulas granting the acordada wide authority. At the same time the crown reaffirmed the tribunal's complete independence of any review or appeal authority other than the viceroy, and once again ordered the criminal court to abstain from interfering with or delaying the operations of the acordada. The continuing inability of the sala del crimen to control effectively the disorders within Mexico City made such a decision almost inevitable.[10]

In 1781 the intensification of efforts to control the carrying of prohibited small arms provided another excuse to oppose the tribunal. The prohibition against carrying such arms did not exclude judicial officers, an omission that again gave the sala del crimen an opportunity to harass the agency. An agent of the sala arrested an acordada member, who had just previously assisted in conducting a notorious criminal to the tribunal's prison, for possession of illegal weapons. The judge of the acordada immediately demanded that the accused be transferred to the tribunal's prison, a demand that the sala ignored on the grounds the judge had no legal right to try his own dependents. The acordada at that time was under an interim judge and consequently not in the best defensive position. The following year Santa María assumed the direction of the tribunal as its permanent judge. He noted that the viceroy had authority to make exceptions in the matter of carrying small arms, as had already been done in the case of the dependents of the royal tobacco monopoly, and pressed for the same privileges for the acordada.[11] Although official sanction apparently was not granted, Santa María forced the sala to stop this particular type of harassment.

The sala del crimen actively contested the right of the acordada to try its own dependents, maintaining correctly that it did not have a statute that permitted such a privilege. The tribunal did not claim such a statutory privilege, but simply proceeded as if it existed. During Aristimuño's tenure as judge the arrest of two acordada members by sala del crimen agents during a raid on a gambling game raised the issue of such privilege. The two arrested agents claimed to be engaged in tracing a horse thief. The acordada tried unsuccessfully to have the two agents transferred to its own authority. In 1784 Santa María attempted to have a case involving a member of the guarda mayor de caminos transferred to his authority on the grounds that members of the guarda enjoyed military privileges. The viceroy ruled against Santa María's request.[12] In another case the judge proceeded to try one of his own dependents for severing someone's hand. Meanwhile, the sala, tracking down the offender, found him in the acordada's prison. The sala received jurisdiction even though sentence had been passed and the case was being reviewed by the junta of revisions.[13] In another instance the viceroy appeared to permit a limited exemption to the acordada, which involved an agent who delivered a suspect to the local prison with excessive violence, only to be arrested by local judicial authorities. Viceregal authorities tranferred the case to the jurisdiction of the acordada on the grounds that the agent had been engaged in the legal exercise of his duties.[14] The sala consistently opposed the attempts of the acordada to enjoy a de facto jurisdiction over its agents and it remained a source of contention throughout the entire century.

Both the sala del crimen and the acordada considered a prisoner, once processed, as the property of the processing agency. When such an individual became involved in a new offense, the organization that had previously sentenced him invariably claimed jurisdiction. In order to obstruct processing by another agency, both the acordada and the sala consistently refused to release the prisoner's past records without which he could not be legally sentenced. It often became necessary for the viceroy to order the release of these documents. Their unwillingness to cooperate in this matter sometimes resulted in the accused languishing in prison. The proprietary attitude of the sala resulted in a squabble over who exercised jurisdiction over escapees from presidios. The acordada claimed authority for itself, while the sala insisted that it had the right to resentence escapees originally condemned to presidios. The crown finally made the logical decision: either one could exercise jurisdiction over deserters, regardless of which one handed down the original sentence, noting that cases of desertion occurred so frequently that as many agents as possible should be empowered to apprehend the deserters.

While the sala del crimen of the audiencia of Mexico proved to be the most troublesome and consistent opponent, the audiencia of Guadalajara also resisted the tribunal. For most of the century the audiencia contented itself with minor harassments—for example, when local acordada agents brought prisoners to the Guadalajara jail, the audiencia accepted them in accordance with regulations but refused to support them, claiming that the tribunal had to bear the expense.[15] The subtle tactics employed by the audiencia of Guadalajara proved hard to defeat. By limiting its cooperation to a bare minimum, it satisfied the letter of the law while still obstructing the tribunal's activities. The viceroy's secretary noted that Martínez required the full support of the viceroy or he would be resisted "principally [by] the audiencia of Guadalajara."[16] Santa María, less than enthusiastic about the attitude of the audiencia, observed that it showed little favor toward his organization.

In the last decade of the century the audiencia of Guadalajara made a determined effort to secure a separate acordada for the kingdom of New Galicia, which would be wholly independent of the tribunal in Mexico but subordinated to the president of the audiencia of Guadalajara. The audiencia even presented a volunteer for the position of judge who indicated his willingness to serve without compensation. In addition it requested permission to amplify the powers of ordinary justices to permit them to execute sentences in robbery cases without prior approval except in the event that the sentence involved mutilation.[17] Robbery was one of the major offenses processed by the acordada under the jurisdiction of the hermandad, and to have approved such an amplification of the powers of an ordinary judicial officer would have led inevitably to conflict between them. The crown refused both proposals, however, observing that no fundamental reason for a separate organization existed.[18] The episode represented an unsuccessful effort by the audiencia of Guadalajara to bring the acordada in New Galicia under its control.

Apart from the sala del crimen in Mexico and the audiencia of Guadalajara, the judge had to contend with the opposition, often physical, of almost every type of judicial officer from intendant down to the local alcalde ordinario, and in some instances of aroused local inhabitants. It was not always a question of justice that aroused such opposition but many times simply resentment of the acordada's independence from local authority.

The jurisdictional conflicts built into the Spanish legal system provided innumerable pretexts for local officials to obstruct the operations of the tribunal. The alcalde mayor of Córdova did not hesitate to imprison three agents with the flimsy excuse that they had invaded his jurisdiction.[19] The alcalde mayor of San Luis de la Paz consistently prevented acordada agents from searching for prohibited liquor in his territory.[20] On the doubtful grounds that an agent had failed to show the proper respect, a local judicial officer ordered his imprisonment. The acordada agent boldly entered the village at the height of the celebration of the village's patron saint and after observing various violations of the prohibited liquor laws, as well as other offenses, he was on the verge of taking action when he was seized.[21] In another case officials of a village municipal council dared to physically prevent an agent of the acordada from administering legally sanctioned punishment.[22]

In some instances local authorities contested the tribunal's legal jurisdiction over delinquents even when the offense obviously fell within the scope of the acordada. The alcalde mayor of Cholula contested the authority of the lieutenant of Puebla in a robbery case which also involved illegal weapons—two offenses unquestionably within the tribunal's jurisdiction.[23] On occasion local officials refused to recognize an agent's commission, or a new official would insist the commission had to be presented to him again in the proper form.[24] The subdelagado of Antigua Vera Cruz refused to recognize a legally presented commission on the grounds that the person holding it was not qualified and had not observed sufficient respect.[25]

The demands of the tribunal for assistance without compensation caused many disputes. Regulations required local authorities to receive acordada prisoners and to maintain and to guard them at their expense, while being deprived of any legal jurisdiction over them. Agents could also require local authorities or landholders to supply men at their expense to conduct prisoners to the prison in Mexico City.[26] The frequency of such demands on the local authorities or inhabitants became a constant source of friction. The local hacendados of the Río Verde district complained that not only did prisoner escorts impose a burdensome expense but diverted men from agricultural duties; in a period of one year they had supplied six such escorts.[27] Opposition to the demands of the acordada took the form of very limited cooperation or of outright refusal to receive its prisoners. The local justice of Pátzquaro once flatly refused to receive prisoners. The subdelegado of Cuautla received prisoners but insisted the acordada provide the necessary guards, and in the subsequent confusion fourteen escaped.[28] The quality of assistance provided often left much to be desired. When agents demanded physical assistance, officials often responded by assigning the dregs of the community, whose absence would not impose an economic hardship on the local merchants or hacendados. The acordada rightfully complained that such people could not be expected to be reliable escorts for prisoners. Spaniards tended to avoid such duties and the burden usually fell on the long-suffering Indians, causing the viceroy to order that both Indians and Spaniards share these tasks.[29]

The opposition of local authorities stemmed from a general resentment of special jurisdictions that inevitably weakened their authority and prestige. Out of a feeling of frustration, many officials reacted by obstructing the acordada's administration of justice. The fact that its agents were not limited to one particular district and could operate freely in any part of the viceroyalty compounded such feelings. Local officials found it doubly galling to have a complete stranger dispensing justice in their district without the necessity of obtaining their permission. It is not surprising then that the tribunal's agents were not greeted with open arms.

At times acordada agents faced the opposition of an entire village, as in the case of the inhabitants of an Indian village in New Galicia who rioted to prevent the arrest of a robbery suspect.[30] The alcalde mayor of Otumba expressed less violent opposition when he complained on behalf of the entire village about the conduct of a local agent. The alcalde observed that the village inhabitants had always obeyed the orders of the acordada with "total resignation" but in this instance felt that a protest was justified. The complaint centered on the alleged misconduct of an agent who, instead of cleaning the roads of bandits, had taken to cleaning the purses of those who passed in front of his dwelling. The alcalde accused the agent of threatening the local inhabitants with arrest unless they met his demands.[31]

Conflict with military authorities was usually initiated by the acordada, which constantly refused to acknowledge the existence of the military's privileged position. Such conflicts often involved violation of the prohibited liquor laws. It will be recalled that the prohibited liquor regulations, which governed the operation of the juzgado de bebidas prohibidas, voided all judicial exemptions, with the sole exception of the ecclesiastical. Thus, in theory, violations of the liquor regulations by soldiers could not be exclusively processed by military courts. In actual practice such a policy proved difficult to enforce.

After the Seven Years' War the crown became vitally concerned with the defense of New Spain. To make service in the regular army and in the militia units more attractive, the crown granted military courts wide jurisdictional control over offenses committed by members of military units. Unfortunately, insufficiently detailed statutes created a general uncertainty concerning the exact extent of military privileges, especially those extended to militia units.[32] Conflict between military courts and other jurisdictions, including the tribunal of the acordada, resulted from the confusion. The acordada charged that many soldiers openly violated the prohibited liquor laws under the protection of the military fuero. Such abuses led Pedro de Valiente, who served as judge from 1778 to 1781, to demand that a decision be made whether or not military privileges exempted offenders against the prohibited liquor regulations from acordada action.[33] In spite of many requests for clarification, the question remained unresolved. In 1784 Santa María noted that soldiers, protected by military authorities, caused frequent disorders in Puebla. The judge complained that military officials dealt far too leniently with their personnel; often soldiers simply spent a few days in prison.[34]

Finally, on February 9, 1793, the crown issued a decree intended to clarify the privileges of the military and to put on end to the numerous jurisdictional disputes between military courts and other agencies. The decree did indeed define the privileges of the regular army, but the question of what privileges extended to the militia units remained to be settled, and consequently jurisdictional disputes continued to disturb the orderly application of justice. The acordada also clashed with the merchants' militia regiment in Mexico City over the intent of the decree of 1793. Santa María, then judge of the tribunal, arrested a soldier of the militia regiment for a violation of the prohibited liquor regulations. In the subsequent squabble with military authorities, Santa María complained that members of the militia erroneously believed themselves protected from the acordada by the decree of 1793. As evidence of their disrespect for the law, he cited the use of prohibited liquors in three wine shops owned by militia members.[35] Conflict between the military and the acordada over prohibited liquor ended only with the legalization of such beverages.

In the end, disputes involving the acordada usually had to be settled by the viceroy. The attitude of the viceroy was therefore extremely important. In the struggle for the viceroy's ear, the tribunal wasted little time. It had become customary for the acordada to escort persons of note to and from the seaports. Although the sala attempted to halt the practice, newly appoined viceroys could count on the judge of the acordada being on hand at Vera Cruz to safely convey the viceregal entourage to the capital and at the same time impress upon it the value of his services. In the early days there was little question that the tribunal enjoyed the full support of the viceroy. As internal order appeared less critical, viceregal support could not be wholly taken for granted. The Conde de Revilla Gigedo, fearful that past disorder would be forgotten, warned his successor to "above all conserve and protect José Velázquez."[36] The secretary to the viceroy, who because of the death of that official prepared the instructions for the new viceroy, noted that the acordada was "as odious as useful."[37] Viceroy Matías de Gálvez observed that such a useful and zealous tribunal had to be respected and dismissed the opposition of various local officials as merely contributing to civil disorder.[38] Viceroy Bucareli consistently supported the acordada, as previously noted. The second Conde de Revilla Gigedo, however, would have preferred the extinction of the acordada, and observed that if the ordinary tribunals functioned on the proper footing the tribunal would not be necessary.[39] Subsequently, the viceroy took steps to increase the efficiency of these tribunals and claimed some limited success. Revilla Gigedo's attitude, and his consequent attempt to revise the acordada's jurisdiction, eventually precipitated an open struggle between the tribunal and the viceroy. The outcome of this struggle fully reaffirmed the acordada and demonstrated the pressure it could bring to bear on the viceroy when he forgot that order had the highest priority.

A jurisdictional dispute between the subdelegado of Xilotepec and the acordada again brought the viceroy and the tribunal into conflict. Revilla Gigedo correctly decided that most of these jurisdictional disputes resulted from the absence of territorial restrictions on individual agents of the tribunal. Agents could descend unknown and unannounced on any area. To eliminate this troublesome aspect of the acordada's administration of justice, Revilla Gigedo ordered that henceforth commissions must limit an agent to his district of residence. In cases when a suspect crossed into another territory he could be apprehended but must be turned over to the agent in that district or to local judicial authorities. The order in effect limited the acordada's territorial jurisdiction so that it was the same as that of ordinary justices.

Santa María jumped to the defense of the unlimited jurisdictional authority of the acordada in a "reverent" protest that contained eighty-seven numbered paragraphs. In this letter the judge noted that regular methods had never been effective in New Spain. He then proceeded to outline the history of the acordada and the reason for its many privileges, noting that the government found it in its interest to protect not restrict the tribunal. Santa María observed that delinquents tended to flee to areas where they were unknown. Consequently, limiting agents to fixed jurisdiction's would make their apprehension unlikely. Where prohibited liquors were concerned, Santa María observed that agents operating out of Mexico had been responsible for the destruction of illegal production of such liquors in Cuernavaca, and if they were now to be restricted to one jurisdiction, such effective surprise sweeps would be impossible. Looking into the future, Santa María predicted an increasingly inactive persecution of criminals and the mass resignations of frustrated agents. Santa María pointed out that the area of Xochimilco, just outside Mexico City, had already become a center for the manufacture and distribution of illegal liquors because of the limitations imposed by the viceroy.[40]

Responding to Santa María's complaints, the viceroy modified the territorial restrictions to permit the judge, with the special permission of the viceroy, to extend commissions to operate outside the fixed jurisdiction for specific cases. But such a modification did not lessen the pressure. Finally, Revilla Gigedo issued a circular dated December 21, 1792, which announced that the order of November 18, 1791, should not be interpreted as limiting the tribunal's authority. Revilla Gigedo declared that the judge had the authority to confer special commissions on agents to operate in other districts. This circular, freely interpreted by Santa María, would have resulted in a return to the unlimited territorial jurisdiction enjoyed prior to 1791. The judge would have to simply supply the necessary documentation to his subordinates to that effect. Santa María, however, refused to be placated by anything less than a full retreat by the viceroy and continued to evoke dark pictures of a return to the disorders of "the first twenty years of the century."[41] Santa María's own statistics did not support such a dire prophecy. His figures indicated that the tribunal successfully apprehended 239 gangs composed of 1,122 individuals in the two-year period between 1792 and 1794.[42] Armed gangs supposedly would have been the first to take advantage of the jurisdictional limitations.

With the replacement of Revilla Gigedo by the Marqués de Branciforte, Santa María moved to eliminate the last vestiges of Revilla Gigedo's restrictions. Calling the Marqués' attention to the regulations, the judge noted that many of the conditions that prompted the creation of the acordada still existed and, to add a note of urgency, expressed the opinion that crime had actually increased because of the former viceroy's attitude. Apparently the Marqués de Branciforte required little urging, and on May 1, 1795, the viceroy revoked the orders issued by Revilla Gigedo. Santa María expressed great satisfaction and offered his humble thanks on behalf of himself and the rest of His Majesty's faithful vassals, noting that he had begun the process of reversing the unfortunate effect of the restrictions.[43]

Thus, for all its wide powers and fearsome reputation, the acordada did not range unchallenged up and down the width and breath of the viceroyalty. At the slightest opportunity, its opponents leaped to the attack. The tribunal in effect operated in potentially hostile territory. The continued necessity, however, for a judicial organization without burdensome political obligations, and the territorial limitations that accompanied them, guaranteed its existence. Although never more than temporarily successful, the constant attacks did serve to inhibit the acordada's application of police powers.

7 THE LAST DECADE

The acordada entered the nineteenth century showing its age. Although the tribunal had successfully warded off the attacks of its opponents, the constant pressure had taken its toll. To protect itself, the acordada had been forced to undercut many of the objections to its methods by supplying the remedies demanded by others. The regulations of 1776 caused a noticeable increase in the amount of paperwork and, subsequently, documentation of its sentences to satisfy the junta of revisions accentuated the trend. Inevitably, the tribunal lost the flexibility that characterized its earlier years. The judge began the nineteenth century virtually a prisoner in his own jail, surrounded and chained to his desk by constant paperwork; only rarely was he able to break away for active duty outside Mexico City.[1]

The acordada's organizational structure became increasingly outmoded. One major jurisdiction, that of the guarda major de caminos, had become entirely atrophied, while another, the juzgado de bebidas prohibidas, had only minimal justification for its continued existence. Only the hermandad remained fully operational. The office of the guarda mayor de caminos had remained unchanged since 1746. The same number of dependents and the same fixed guardhouses were in use in 1800.

While the guarda had remained static, however, the road system had not. In 1803 Baron Alexander von Humboldt noted that six major roads linked the valley of Mexico with the rest of New Spain, including the two major links with the city of Puebla.[2] Mexico City had become the hub of innumerable roads radiating in every direction and completely bypassing the fixed guardhouses. Even though the guardhouses were of doubtful effectiveness, they continued in operation, draining funds and energy without much return. Their decreasing importance led to physical neglect and the judge of the acordada was understandably reluctant to divert funds for their renovation and repair. The physical conditions of the posts finally forced the issue into the open. Faced with the complete collapse of one such structure, the judge requested special funds to rebuild it, estimating the cost at one thousand pesos. The final cost, however, exceeded five thousand pesos. To add to the problem, the new building proved to be defective, resulting in extremely critical comments. Viceregal authorities ordered the judge to inspect all the guardhouses and report those that warranted reconstruction. In the course of the inspection Santa María concluded that the guarda, hopelessly outmoded, served no useful purpose. He recommended the closing of such fixed posts and diversion of the funds to increase the salaries and help defray the costs of certain other dependents, principally the lieutenants of Oaxaca, Vera Cruz, Guadalajara, and Puebla. Puebla would receive the largest share of the funds since, as Santa María observed, it had become the "throat through which passed innumerable people of all classes."[3] In spite of Santa María's irrefutable logic, the viceroy did not take any action.

While the guarda mayor de caminos had become a useless limb, the juzgado de bebidas prohibidas had also lost much of its justification for existence. The juzgado had at best been minimally effective. The need for new sources of revenue added incentive to the reconsideration of the entire policy of suppression of illegal liquors. As early as 1776 the crown legalized cane brandy in the province of Yucatán in order to raise the necessary revenue to support the regular troops and the militia.[4] In 1780 mescal was legalized in the *provincias internas*, and the subsequent revenue applied to public works. Such revenue amounted to 24,319.5.6 pesos in 1792.[5] Finally, in 1796 cane brandy was legalized in the entire viceroyalty.[6] Mescal would not be legalized in the rest of the viceroyalty until 1811.[7] Cane brandy had always been the principal prohibited liquor competing with the legal beverages. Its legalization all but eliminated the necessity for maintaining the juzgado de bebidas prohibidas.

As has been previously noted, the juzgado had become the acordada's financial backbone. To remove the jurisdiction of the juzgado without finding alternate financial support would have resulted in the tribunal's destruction. The acordada's structure had become so outmoded that it required all the energy of Santa María to keep it operating. It clearly required major reorganization. The dead limbs of the guarda mayor de caminos and the juzgado de bebidas prohibidas needed to be removed. Such a reorganization, however, had to be accomplished without destroying the organization's financial base. The viceregal authorities preferred avoiding this major task and the juzgado de bebidas prohibidas remained a part of the organization to the very end.

In addition to organizational problems, the crown's desire to achieve the utmost police control at the least cost conflicted with the increased demand for more formal justice. The crown could not have formal justice at volunteer prices. The volume of paper work had reached the stage where the staff worked even on official holidays to control the flood of documents. The judge noted that although the salary of the clerical staff seemed very attractive the volume of work made prospective employees "look with horror" at the very idea of working at the acordada.[8] The organization's administration rapidly approached a critical point. Santa María's death in 1808 may have sparked the decline. The problems that had been building up could hardly continue to be held at bay even by exceptional talent and energy.

With the appointment of Antonio Columna as successor to Santa María, some reorganization appeared inevitable. The crown seriously considered separation from the acordada of the guarda mayor de caminos. When Columna became judge, he received only an interim appointment as head of the juzgado de bebidas prohibidas, the guarda mayor de caminos, and the hermandad. Apparently the crown contemplated a major reorganization of these jurisdictions.[9]

Unfortunately, circumstances did not permit the acordada to resolve its organizational problems. Events in Spain had already intervened to change the state of affairs in Mexico. The same year Santa María died, the French imprisoned the Spanish king, and the government of Spain soon fell into the hands of his increasingly liberal-minded subjects. This grave situation naturally pushed such questions as the acordada's reorganization off the agenda. In 1809 the central junta in Spain dispatched an order to New Spain calling for the strictest economies in government and the elimination of all unnecessary positions.[10] Again the question of the suppression of the juzgado de bebidas prohibidas was examined, and again the obvious dependence of the entire tribunal of the acordada on the funds of the juzgado blocked any reorganization.

Beginning in 1810 New Spain was confronted by an armed insurrection. The growing insecurity of the royal highways, which were plagued by a mixture of bandits and insurgents, prompted the viceroy to order Columna to devise some plan to control the main roads out of Mexico City. Columna worked out a scheme to divide the most important routes into sections, each under the command of a reliable lieutenant supported by the necessary manpower. The road from Otumba to Buena Vista, virtually blocked by a bandit gang of seventy men, would be cleared and guarded by a lieutenant and thirty men. Under the lieutenant of Puebla two patrols a week would secure the road to Mexico City. The main route north and the road to Toluca were similarly divided into sections and assigned to lieutenants. The viceroy, with the approval of the *junta de seguridad y buen orden*, bestowed the rank of lieutenant in the militia on the various agents in charge. The men serving under the lieutenants were ranked as sergeants, corporals, and ordinary soldiers, and their units were invested with military privileges, principally because of their contact with armed insurgents.[11] Regular agents of the acordada did not receive such privileges. The highway patrols were to be the organization's only role in quelling the insurrection.

In the midst of the difficult times facing the acordada and the entire viceroyalty, Columna traveled to Spain on private business, leaving his agency in the hands of a temporary substitute. Such a substitution was strictly prohibited for any reason, including prolonged illness, and the fact that Columna illegally left his post was a sign of the acordada's decline.[12] Juan José Flores, who became the interim judge, subsequently succeeded Columna serving as the last judge of the tribunal.

In 1812 mounting insurrection forced the sala del crimen to solidly support the acordada for the first time since its establishment. Ironically, this occurred shortly before the tribunal would be abolished. Too late, the sala supported the reforms that should have been imposed at the turn of the century, if not earlier. The sala urged that the juzgado de bebidas prohibidas be separated from the acordada, without removing the funds necessary for the continued operation of the tribunal until new tax revenues could be assigned. In addition the sala del crimen pressed for a splitting of the acordada into two separate bodies—one in Mexico City, the other in Guadalajara.[13] Their suggestions were not aimed at weakening the organization; rather they wanted to strengthen it so that it could take an active part in suppressing the pillage and violence that inevitably accompanied armed insurrection. Significantly, the sala made no mention of subordinating the proposed reorganized acordada to its own authority. It solemnly noted that the internal situation in the viceroyalty made the acordada even more necessary than the events that had resulted in its creation.

Even as steps were being taken in Mexico to convert the acordada into an anti-insurgent force, events in Spain had already decided the agency's fate. The liberal constitution of 1812 reached Mexico, throwing the legality of the acordada into doubt. This new constitution reorganized the judicial structure both in Spain and in the Spanish possessions in America. A Supreme Tribunal of Justice was created, to which all the audiencias, including those of Mexico and Guadalajara, were subordinated. The audiencias in turn received jurisdiction in the second and third instance over all cases, civil or criminal, within established territorial limits. The new regulations required subordinate justices to advise the audiencia of all cases in progress within a period of three days after official action had commenced, and all cases had to be formulated in a uniform manner.

Prisoners could not be excluded from regular prison inspections under any pretext and the accused had the right to be advised of the reason for his arrest within twenty hours after being seized. No tribunal would be permitted to issue any separate regulations concerning the administration of justice.[14]

The acordada's operations directly conflicted with the constitution of 1812 on all these points. The audiencia, meeting with the viceroy in consultative session to discuss the application of the new constitution, decided that although there was no specific mention of the tribunal of the acordada, its continued existence appeared incompatible with the new judicial structure.[15] The audiencia cited article 248 which stated that in all matters, civil or criminal, there was to be only one jurisdiction.[16]

It should be noted that the constitution of 1812 as it applied to criminal justice, represented more of a reorganization than a general liberalization of criminal law. Several articles of the new constitution in particular support this opinion. Articles 249 and 250 provided for the continuance of separate ecclesiastical and military jurisdictions in spite of article 248. Moreover, article 278 reserved the right to create special tribunals with their own separate jurisdictions. Prisoners could be held incommunicado at the discretion of judicial authorities under the provisions of article 297. And, finally, article 308 provided that if the security of the state was endangered, the formalities prescribed in criminal cases could be suspended by the Cortes for a determined period in all or part of Spanish territory. The creation of another organization such as the acordada was theoretically possible under the constitution that the audiencia decided demanded the tribunal's abolition.

The suppression of the acordada, however, was not an act of vengeance, nor did it reflect a liberalization of the audiencia's views on the administration of justice. In a country caught in the throes of a violent insurrection, which split all levels of the population into opposing factions, the loyalty of a volunteer organization such as the acordada could not be taken for granted. Antonio Columna had been forced to individually screen agents for loyalty before selecting them for the new road patrols previously mentioned. The tribunal's volunteer agents could not be considered wholly reliable subjects of the king. The audiencia decided that troops rather than the acordada were needed to put down the insurrection and observed that the funds of the tribunal could be better spent for this purpose.[17]

So ended the tribunal of the acordada. A little life still remained in the corpse however. The decree of December 28, 1814, ordering a return of the laws to their position in 1808 followed Ferdinand VII's restoration. In theory the decree automatically reestablished the acordada, but in actuality its funds had already been committed. Even the tribunal's prison, then being used as a tobacco warehouse, was physically unavailable. The incentive to reactivate the acordada proved insufficient to overcome the problems. The viceregal treasury noted that returning the prison to the tribunal would necessitate moving the arms factory from the former tobacco warehouse, and arms, after all, seemed more important than the acordada to "root out the traitors and pacify the kingdom."[18] The inevitable was accepted, and the acordada passed into history.

CONCLUSION

The establishment of the acordada represented a major philosophical advance in the administration of justice in New Spain. It broke sharply and dramatically with the traditional system of limited jurisdictions confined in a suffocating mixture of administrative and judical responsibilities. Excessive concern with political matters had automatically dictated a dispersal of power among a number of officials and institutions, making it difficult to concentrate the energy necessary to regulate an increasingly complex society. The tribunal's creation signaled a change in royal policy. Freed of direct political functions, the acordada concentrated on law enforcement. No other viceregal organization received such specialized powers. Relieved of normal judicial subordination to the sala del crimen, the tribunal imposed and executed sentences. It placed centralized police authority in the hands of the viceroy who alone exercised direct control over the organization's judge and its agents. The formation of the acordada was a positive approach to the problem of regulating society. As such, its creation and subsequent approval by Philip V, first monarch of the new Bourbon dynasty, indicated the growing maturity of Spanish colonial administration. Significantly, the rationalization of law enforcement in New Spain occurred well in advance of the reforms traditionally credited to the Bourbon monarchs, suggesting that evolutionary forces, even in New Spain, may well have been as important as new leadership.

Even though the acordada relied on unpaid volunteers, many of them merchants or landholders and their employees with a vested interest in enforcing the law in their districts, it was not a vigilante organization. The judge in Mexico City individually appointed and removed each agent and required his dependents to keep him informed of all cases in progress. In most instances individuals guilty of major offenses appeared before the judge and

Conclusion

his assessors in the viceregal capital for sentencing. During the tribunal's early existence its procedures tended to be rather informal. After 1756, however, formal instructions were outlined, and in 1776 a comprehensive reglamento brought the agency's administration of justice into line with eighteenth-century standards. Yet, the organization's volunteer nature made it difficult to translate theory into practice and in general worked against professionalism.

The acordada, like the sala del crimen of the audiencia, operated as a reserve system dealing with those crimes that could not be effectively dealt with by local officials in the traditional ad hoc manner. Unlike the sala and other judicial agencies, it did not engage in passive law enforcement. The tribunal, not dependent on local officials to formally refer cases, actively sought out malefactors and brought them to justice. Because the majority of agents served without compensation, the type of criminal activity they were willing to devote their time and energy to suppress was obviously affected. As local landholders, merchants, and other dependents, they had an understandable interest in controlling crimes involving property rather than purely social crimes such as homicide, assault, and sexual offenses, as indicated by the statistics. The interest of the state and such individuals coincided. Banditry, robbery, and theft undermined the authority and prestige of the viceregal government, hindered economic activity with subsequent ill effects on the treasury, and disturbed society in general. With the investment of relatively insignificant state funds to provide an organizational structure for the volunteer agents, the viceregal government demonstrated its ability to confine criminal activity throughout New Spain to an acceptable level.

The difficult question of the justness of the order imposed on the population of New Spain cannot be ignored. Unquestionably the move toward formal procedures was a healthy development and made the attainment of justice more of a possibility. Without a structured application of the law, justice depends on arbitrary whim or wisdom. The elaboration of set procedures and responses that define behavorial limits perhaps is a step toward justice in the ideal sense. The drawing of a line between acceptable and culpable conduct reduces the gray zone between the innocent and the guilty and makes it possible to depersonalize, to a certain degree, the imposition of punishment. Without formalization and

Conclusion

depersonalization, justice remains largely discretionary and abuses of authority may only be checked by a forceful, and often violent, response. Considering that both the acordada and the sala del crimen served as a reserve system, while the principal burden of control lay with local officials, it cannot be claimed that a great movement toward due process and depersonalization had occurred. Yet, the trend had begun.

The correlative question of course is how oppressive was law and order. It is evident that colonial administrators worried over the thin distinction between control and oppression. Clearly different levels of conduct existed; consequently, control over certain groups might well have been considered oppressive if applied to others. In the context of modern racial attitudes the association of certain groups with antisocial behavior is morally indefensible as well as socially oppressive. In New Spain, however, the connection seemed natural in spite of the violence such an attitude did to the self-esteem of certain castes. On another level, it is obvious colonial authorities desired only a certain degree of judicial control which met their conception of the requirements of a politically viable, responsible government. They appeared well aware that the cooperation of the governed could only be elicited not forced. As a consequence, mutually acceptable limits had to be adhered to by the government. Even local administrators functioned on that principle. The alternative was repression, a costly solution that invites rebellion—the bane of all colonial authorities.

The history of the acordada itself reveals the concern of the administrators. Once the disorderly situation had been brought under control, the viceregal government immediately began the task of tempering the methods employed. Creation of the junta of revisions further emphasized the concern of the authorities with the problem of oppression. In addition, the type of punishment imposed, particularly in the latter half of the century, even by today's standards, appears restrained. Laying aside the matter of flogging, one is impressed with the evident moderation in formal punishment. The extremely limited use of capital punishment, the ten-year maximum of presidio terms, and the flexibility between the limits, indeed could provide a model for present-day enforcement systems. The flaw developed during the processing of a case. Faulty collection of evidence, long imprisonment before sentencing, and inability of the accused to influence the course of events made justice extremely one-sided. Very little was done to redress the imbalance between a powerful state and the powerless individual hampered by racial attitudes as well as economic and social disabilities. The accused played a passive role in accepting punishment or benevolence as decided by the authorities. Once an individual's actions had gone beyond the point that could be dealt with by local officials, certain set procedures existed which in effect allowed social resistance to state intervention to be gauged before the final imposition of punishment. Yet, official moderation toward the group did not protect the individual once he was thought to be guilty.

Such a system could be potentially oppressive and in many cases may have been. Concern for the abstract principles of justice, however, was present. The interplay between agencies, local officials, and other components of the viceregal system served to moderate the acordada's impact. Other authorities, often jealous of their own prerogatives, offered both legal and illegal avenues of resistance. More important, they were forced to mobilize their own moral and political constituencies in order to bolster their cause. They justified their opposition in terms of the welfare of the king's subjects rather than narrow and often personal goals that may have been their actual concern. As a result, the concept of justice was stimulated by the rubbing together of a relatively complex bureaucracy.

With independence the impetus for a more enlightened society would pass from crown officials to proponents of nineteenth-century Spanish liberalism and their heirs in New Spain. Although philosophical change did in fact influence the direction of an independent Mexico, many of the same problems remained. A large segment of the population continued to exist on the socioeconomic fringes. In addition, limited financial resources and political instability favored a continuation of the ad hoc enforcement of order at the local level. Nevertheless, the trend toward a formal, salaried police agency with set procedures persisted. The developemnt of a rural police agency under Benito Juárez and Sebastián Lerdo de Tejada which evolved into the *rurales*, in essence followed the direction of law enforcment established during the eighteenth century.[1] The recognition of the state of the need to demonstrate its ability to guarantee a degree of order in a regulated and formal manner owed much to the colonial experience, as well as to immediate events. The abuses associated with the rurales during the *pax porfiriana* that preceded the revolution of 1910 resulted from social and institutional conditions that would have been understood by the judges of the acordada. Time and progress have not modified the Mexican environment beyond the context of its colonial legacy.

APPENDIX TABLES

APPENDIX TABLES

TABLE 1
JUDGES OF THE ACORDADA AND SENTENCES IMPOSED BY THEM

(Based on documents in the section of the acordada, *AGN*; the quantities vary somewhat in several reports. Consequently, such figures must be considered approximate indicators.)

Judges and dates of service		Workhouses	Presidios	Executed	Exiled	Died	Temporary confinement or minor punishment	Total
Miguel Velázquez de Lorea*	1703–1732	173	352	146	6	8	96	781
José Velázquez de Lorea	1732–1756	531	1,955	320	24	43	432	3,305
Jacinto Martínez de la Concha	1756–1774	16	3,921	92	1	207	448	4,685
Francisco Antonio Aristimuño	1774–1776	2	780	24	—	18	189	1,013
Juan José Barberi (temporary appointment)	1776–1778	—	378	8	2	8	210	606
Pedro Valiente	1778–1781	—	1,026	37	3	8	693	1,767
Juan José Barberi (temporary appointment)	1781–1782	—	344	3	1	2	170	520
Manuel Antonio de Santa María	1782–1808	257	10,244	246	—	945	30,979	42,671
Antonio Columna	1808–1811	6	340	2	—	42	1,841	2,231
Juan José Flores (not confirmed by the crown)	1811–1813	—	—	—	—	—	—	—

* Includes cases processed before creation of the acordada in his capacity of alcalde provincial de la hermandad.

TABLE 2
PERCENTAGE DISTRIBUTION OF ACORDADA SENTENCES BY RACIAL GROUPS
(Sala del crimen sentences in parenthesis)*

Types of crimes	Spanish	Indian	Mestizo	Mulatto
Homicide	4	11	7	6
	(34)	(85)	(51)	(56)
Assault with bodily injury	4	4	4	6
	(2)	(1)	(1)	(4)
Highway or street robbery	36	38	26	23
	(14)	(3)	(16)	(12)
Theft of livestock	28	26	24	37
	(2)	(1)	(1)	(2)
Vagrancy	3	1	5	7
	(23)	(0)	(17)	(12)
Sexual offenses other than rape	0	0	0	0
	(2)	(5)	(4)	(10)
Breaking and entering	5	4	9	4
	(0)	(0)	(0)	(0)
Pickpocket and minor street theft	6	0	3	6
	(1)	(0)	(1)	(0)
Deserter from presidio	6	6	7	3
	(4)	(1)	(0)	(0)
Rape	2	5	2	2
	(3)	(3)	(6)	(0)
Miscellaneous	6	5	13	6
	(15)	(1)	(3)	(4)

* Tables 2, 3, and 4 are based on 558 presidio sentences imposed by the acordada in 1799 and 1800. Judge Santa María (1782–1808) averaged 394 presidio sentences a year; consequently, 558 cases represent approximately 71% of such sentences over the two-year period. The sala del crimen percentages are derived from 400 cases over the same length of time and probably consist of an even higher percentage of such sentences than those of the acordada.

TABLE 3
Occupation of Those Processed
(All racial groups)

Occupation	Acordada	Sala del crimen
Laborers—rural and urban	25	19
Artisans	23	24
Small farmer or husbandryman	17	18
Service industries—those with some skill but not sufficient to fall into the artisan category	15	14
Without employment or trade (vagrant)	4	5
Supervisory personnel	4	3
Tradesmen, dealers, scribes, and students	4	2
No occupation listed	8	15

TABLE 4
Percentage Processed by Racial Classification

Race	Acordada	Sala del crimen	Combined
Indian	29	39	33
Spanish	30	25	28
Mestizo	22	22	22
Mulatto	19	14	17

NOTES

CHAPTER I

[1] The acceptance of the New World's existence involved much more than the report of its "discovery." See Edmundo O'Gorman, *The Invention of America* (Bloomington, 1961). The difficulty of separating the real from the unreal is clearly presented by an actual participant in the conquest. See Bernal Díaz, *Historia verdadera de la conquista de la Nueva España*, 5th ed. (Mexico, 1960).

[2] *Recopilación de leyes de los reynos de las Indias* (Madrid, 1791), lib. 5 tit. 2, ley 24 (hereafter cited as *Recopilación*). In reality it would have been difficult, if not impossible, to have developed common law to meet the fundamentally opposed needs of the conquerors and the conquered. J. H. Parry, *The Spanish Theory of Empire in the Sixteenth Century* (Cambridge, 1940), p. 70.

[3] Special protection also implied diminished responsibility. As a minor an Indian could not present testimony under oath. The testimony of six Indians was deemed equivalent to one Spaniard. John Leddy Phelan, *The Kingdom of Quito in the Seventeenth Century* (Madison, 1967), p. 199.

[4] Parry, *Spanish Theory*, p. 72. The volume of royal legislation made it difficult for officials to organize a coherent enforcement policy. A concise summary of the numerous attempts to gather the laws of the Indies into a workable collection may be found in José María Ots Capdequi, "Las fuentes del derecho indiano," *Humanidades*, XXV, 1 (1936), 23–36.

[5] Antonio Muro Orejón, "Leyes del nuevo código de Indias vigentes en América," *Revista de Indias*, V, 17 (July–September 1944), 444.

[6] *Recopilación*, lib. 2, tit. 1, ley 2. The laws of Toro contain a further ranking as follows: the ordenamiento de Alcalá, municipal fueros, fuero real, and las partidas. José María Ots Capdequi, *España en América; las institucióines coloniales*, 2d ed. (Bogota, 1952), p. 34.

[7] A. H. M. Jones, *Studies in Roman Government and Law* (Oxford, 1960), p. 135.

[8] E. A. Thompson, *The Goths in Spain* (Oxford, 1969), p. 3.

[9] E. N. Van Kleffens, *Hispanic Law Until the End of the Middle Ages* (Edinburgh, 1968), p. 71.

[10] Kenneth L. Karst, *Latin American Legal Institutions: Problems for Comparative Study* (Berkeley and Los Angeles, 1966), p. 124.

[11] Paul Goubert, S. J., "Byzance et l'Espagne wisigothique (554–711)" *Études Byzantines*, II (1944), 75.

[12] S. P. Scott, *History of the Moorish Empire in Europe* (Philadelphia, 1904), III, 183.

[13] Clifford Stevens Walton, *The Civil Law in Spain and Spanish America* (Washington, D.C., 1900), p. 65.

[14] Karst, *Latin American Legal Institutions*, p. 124.

[15] The partidas marked an important point in the struggle between Roman and Germanic law in Spain. Charles Sumner Lobingier, "Las Siete Partidas and its Predecessors," *California Law Review*, I (1913), 491.

[16] "Ordenamiento de Alcalá," *Los códigos Españoles concordados y anotados*, Vol. I, tit. 28 (Madrid, 1847), p. 462.

[17] Roger Bigelow Merriman, *The Rise of the Spanish Empire in the Old World and the New* (New York, 1962), I, 229.

[18] *Ibid.*, p. 230.

[19] *Ibid.*, p. 231.

[20] *Ibid.*, p. 233.

[21] Julio Puyol Alonso, *Las hermandades de Castilla y León* (Madrid, 1913), p. 11.

[22] Marvin Lunenfeld *The Council of the Santa Hermandad: A Study of the Pacification Forces of Ferdinand and Isabella* (Coral Gables, 1970), p. 55.

[23] *Ibid.*, p. 58.

[24] *Ibid.*, p. 54.

[25] J. H. Elliot, *Imperial Spain, 1464–1716* (London, 1963), p. 76.

[26] Merriman, *Rise of the Spanish Empire*, II, 122.

[27] *Ibid.*, p. 147.

[28] *Ibid.*, p. 125.

[29] Ots Capdequi, *España en América*, p. 34.

[30] Carl Ortwin Sauer, *The Early Spanish Main* (Berkeley and Los Angeles, 1969), p. 196.

[31] A fact made abundantly evident when he returned from Spain in 1530 only to have the audiencia bar him from the city he had conquered under pain of the loss of his property and the "pleasure of the king." Francisco López de Gómara, *Cortés: The Life of the Conqueror by His Secretary*, trans. Lesley Byrd Simpson (Berkeley and Los Angeles, 1965), p. 395.

[32] The strength, as well as weakness, of the Indian political and social structure is clearly presented in R. C. Padden, *The Hummingbird and the Hawk* (New York, 1970), and in a more sympathetic fashion by Jacques Soustelle, *The Daily Life of the Aztecs on the Eve of the Spanish Conquest* (Stanford, 1970).

[33] Gonzalo Aguirre Beltrán, "El gobierno indígena en México y el proceso de aculturación," *América indígena*, XII, 4 (October 1952), 272.

[34] Robert S. Chamberlain, "The Concept of the Señor Natural as Revealed by Castilian Law and Administrative Documents," *Hispanic American Historical Review*, XIX, 2 (May 1939), 132.

[35] The rapid and disastrous decline of the Indian population in the Antilles convinced the crown that Indian labor represented the true wealth of the colonies and its exploitation had to be controlled. A vivid picture of the disaster is presented by Sauer, *Early Spanish Main*, pp. 200–207.

[36] Lesley Byrd Simpson, *The Encomienda in New Spain* (Berkeley and Los Angeles, 1950), p. 62.

[37] Charles Gibson, *The Aztecs Under Spanish Rule* (Stanford, 1964), p. 60.

[38] Simpson, *Encomienda*, p. 115.

[39] Luis Gonzáles Obregón, *Rebeliónes indígenas y precursores de la independencia Mexicana en los siglos, XVI, XVII, y XVIII*, 2d ed., rev. (Mexico, 1952), p. 456.

[40] López-Portillo, in somewhat an overstatement, noted that had the revolt

succeeded in Mexico, Spain could not have held Peru or the areas in between the two principal bastions of Spanish power. Thus, victory assured the spread of European culture in the New World. José López-Portillo y Weber, *La rebelión de Nueva Galicia* (Mexico, 1939), p. 593.

41 Simpson, *Encomienda*, p. 140.

42 Gibson, *Aztecs Under Spanish Rule*, p. 62.

43 A complete account of the conspiracy as well as a number of the major documents may be found in Manuel Orozco y Berra, *Noticia histórica de la conjuración del Marqués del Valle. Años de 1565–1568* (Mexico, 1853).

44 The crown dispatched two other *jueces pesquisidores* with Muñoz, one died enroute and the other, Dr. Luis Carrillo, appears to have been overshadowed by his more energetic colleague. Orozco y Berra, *Noticia histórica*, p. 58. The encomenderos might well have developed into a privileged military caste except for their obvious reluctance to engage in distant and costly campaigns. They enjoyed the status and military trapping, but without professional dedication. Lyle N. McAlister, "Social Structure and Social Change in New Spain," *Hispanic American Historical Review*, XLIII, 3 (August 1963), 360.

CHAPTER II

1 Even the viceroy's salary was listed as a judicial expense. Joaquín Maniau, *Compendio de la historia de la real hacienda de Nueva España* (Mexico, 1914), p. 44.

2 The need for expanded powers was well recognized. Juan de Solórzano Pereira, *Política indiana* (Madrid, 1736), lib. V, cap. 3, num. 10.

3 José María Ots Capdequi, *Institucónes* (Barcelona, 1959), p. 258.

4 José Antonio Calderón Quijano, *Los virreyes de Nueva España en el reinado de Carlos III* (Sevilla, 1968), I, 251.

5 John Leddy Phelan, *The Kingdom of Quito in the Seventeenth Century* (Madison, 1967), p. 197.

6 Different regulations (ordinance of Monzón, 1562) governed the operations of audiencias located outside the viceregal capitals. For an account of the operations of a provincial audiencia see J. H. Parry, *The Audiencia of New Galicia in the Sixteenth Century* (Cambridge, 1968).

7 Solórzano Pereira, *Política indiana*, lib. V, cap. 3, num. 7.

8 Eusebio Ventura Beleña, *Recopilación sumaria de todos los autos acordadas de la real audiencia y sala del crimen de Nueva España* (Mexico, 1787), I, 66.

9 Phelan, *Kingdom of Quito*, p. 127.

10 *Instruccónes que los virreyes de Nueva España dejaron a sus sucesores* (Mexico, 1873), I, 237 (hereafter cited as *Instruccónes*).

11 Some confusion exists as to the differences between the two officials. Solórzano Pereira (*Política indiana*, lib. 5, cap. 2, num. 1) reported that the title *corregidor* was used in Peru while that of *alcalde mayor* applied in New Spain. Differences, however, between them have been noted. Charles Gibson, *The Aztecs Under Spanish Rule* (Stanford, 1964), p. 487 n. 98. In the eighteenth century approximately half the corregidores assigned to Indian towns violated the law and neglected their political and judicial duties by residing in Mexico City. *Ibid.*, p. 95. In addition, their trading activities often became a primary concern. See Brian R. Hamnett, *Politics and Trade in Southern*

Mexico (Cambridge, 1971).

[12] John Preston Moore, *The Cabildo in Peru Under the Hapsburgs* (Durham, 1954), p. 103.

[13] Solórzano Pereira, *Política indiana*, lib. V, cap. 1, num. 14.

[14] Calderón Quijano, *Los virreyes de Nueva España*, II, 255.

[15] *Ibid.*, p. 265. Earlier divisions in 1694, 1713, 1720, and 1750 had proven ineffective. Alicia Bazán Alarcón, "El Real Tribunal de la Acordada y la delincuencia en la Nueva España" (Tesis, maestra de historia de México, Universidad Nacional Autonoma de Mexico (Mexico, 1963), pp. 14, 85.

[16] Gonzalo Aguirre Beltrán, "El gobierno indígena en México y el proceso de aculturación," *América indígena*, XII (October 1952), 282.

[17] Luis Chávez Orozco, *Las institucíones democráticas de los indígenas mexicanos en la época colonial* (Mexico, 1942), p. 6.

[18] C. H. Haring, *The Spanish Empire in America* (New York, 1963), p. 56. The simplified appeals process of the juzgado represented a genuine attempt to protect the Indian's right of redress from becoming a victim of the legal complexity of Spanish law. Apparently, its services were used extensively. Woodrow Borah, "Social Welfare and Social Obligation in New Spain: A Tentative Assessment," XXXVI Congreso Internacional de Americanistas. *Actas y Memorias* (Sevilla, 1966), IV, 55.

[19] Norman F. Martin, *Los vagabundos en la Nueva España siglo XVI* (Mexico, 1957), p. 63. Thomas Gage, on English priest who traveled through Mexico in the first half of the seventeenth century, reported that a "whole [Indian] town standeth in awe of one Spaniard." Eric S. Thompson, ed., *Thomas Gage's Travels in the New World* (Norman, Okla., 1958), p. 22.

[20] Richard M. Morse, "Some Characteristics of Latin American Urban History," *American Historical Review*, LXVII, 2 (January 1962), 335.

[21] Haring, *Spanish Empire*, p. 123. Viceroy Luis de Velasco (1550-1564) conferred the hermandad's functions on the two alcaldes of the *mesta* (grazer's guild in Mexico City. Other representatives of the mesta probably received the same responsibilities. Herbert Ingram Priestly, *The Mexican Nation, A History* (New York, 1923), p. 76.

[22] *Recopilación*, lib. 5, tit. 4, ley 1, and lib. 5, tit. 3, ley 18.

[23] Woodrow Borah, *New Spain's Century of Depression* (Berkeley and Los Angeles, 1951), p. 27.

[24] Gibson, *Aztecs Under Spanish Rule*, p. 242. For an excellent discussion of *obraje* labor, see Richard E. Greenleaf, "The Obraje in the Late Mexican Colony," *The Americas*, XXIII, 3 (January 1967), 227-250.

[25] The municipal government had discussed the establishment of a granary in 1537, but conditions evidently were not sufficently pressing to stimulate action. Raymond L. Lee, "Grain Legislation in Colonial Mexico, 1575-1585," *Hispanic American Historical Review*, XXVII, 4 (November 1947), 655.

[26] Chester Lyle Guthrie, "Riots in Seventeenth Century Mexico City: A Study of Social and Economic Conditions," *Greater America, Essays in Honor of Herbert Eugene Bolton* (Berkeley and Los Angeles, 1945), p. 245.

[27] Borah, *New Spain's Century of Depression*, p. 25.

[28] Antonio de Robles, *Diario de sucesos notables* (1665-1703) (colección de escritores Mexicanos (Mexico, 1946), I, 225.

[29] Juan Francisco Gemelli Carreri, *Las cosas más considerables vistas en la Nueva España* (Mexico, 1946), p. 126.

[30] *Ibid.*, p. 132.

[31] Guthrie, "Riots," p. 246.

[32] Robles, *Diario*, II, 242.
[33] Carlos de Sigüenza y Góngora, *Alboroto y motín de México del 8 de junio de 1692* (Mexico, 1932), p. 70.
[34] The uprising in Tlaxcala involved the Indians of Santa Cruz. Loyal Indians put the revolt down and the four hundred troops sent by the governor of Vera Cruz on the viceroy's order proved unnecessary. In nearby Puebla, all Spaniards fifteen years and over received weapons, and guards were placed in all public buildings. Such measures averted serious disorders in the city. Antonio Carrión, *Historia de la cuidad de la Puebla de los Angeles* (Puebla, 1896), II, 36.
[35] Robles, *Diario*, II, 259.
[36] Chester Lyle Guthrie, "Colonial Economy, Trade, Industry and Labor in Seventeenth Century Mexico City," *Revista de historia de América*, no. 7 (1939), p. 133.
[37] Robles, *Diario* II, 258.
[38] In 1695 the sala del crimen ordered all vagrants to find employment within one month or face being exiled to the Philippines, Robles, *Diario*, III, 32. In 1710 the audiencia of New Galicia instructed the municipal council of Zacatecas to appoint the first alcalde judge of vagabonds when he retired from the council as a result of normal municipal elections. Elias Amador, *Bosquejo histórico de Zacatecas* (Zacatecas, 1892), p. 446.
[39] Guthrie, "Colonial Economy," p. 118.
[40] Jesús Romero Flores, *México-historia de una gran cuidad* (Mexico, 1953), p. 322.
[41] Lucas Alamán, *Historia de Méjico* (Mexico, 1849), I, 53.
[42] Francisco Sedaño, *Noticias de México* (Mexico, 1880), I, 8.
[43] Beleña, *Recopilación sumaria*, I, 70. Such decisive action was made possible by a royal cédula of December 21, 1715, which authorized the formation of a junta, under viceregal direction, to consider the problem of order and implement remedies, Alicia Bazán Alarcón, "El Real Tribunal de la Acordada y la delincuencia en la Nueva España," *Historia Mexicana*, XIII, 3 (Enero-Marzo, 1964), 324.
[44] *Archivo general de la Nación* cédulas, Vol. XLIII, exp. 23 (hereafter cited as *AGN*).
[45] Sedaño, *Noticias*, I, 9.
[46] Diego Antonio de Escobar, *Sermón epidictico... hizo el día 22 de septembre de este año de 1732... al Capp^n D. Miguel Velásquez Lorea....* (Mexico, 1732).
[47] Diego Panes y Abellán, *Cronología de los vireyes... de esta Nueva España....* (Mexico, n.d.).
[48] Luis Velasco y Mendoza, *Historia de la cuidad de Celaya* (Mexico, 1947), I, 171.
[49] Ignacio Espinoza de los Monteiros, *Oración continua fúnebre... hizo el día 17 de mayo de este año de 1756... al... Joseph Velázquez Lorea...* (Mexico, 1756), p. 263.
[50] El Señor Santa María
tiene que hacer una casa
ya Piedra y Paredes tiene
Madera solo le falta

Bancroft notes that Santa María was pursuing a bandit named Pillo Madera; however, Madera had been captured by Jacinto Martínez de la Concha, a previous judge. Both feats were combined in this popular song. Hubert Howe

Bancroft, *History of Mexico* (San Francisco, 1886), III, 274.
⁵¹ *AGN*, Acordada, XV, 66.
⁵² Pasajero: respeta este edificio
y procura evitar su triste entrada
pues cerrada una vez su dura puerta
solo para el suplicio se halla abierta.
Artemio de Valle-Arispe, *Historia de la cuidad de México*, 4th ed. (Mexico, 1946), p. 469.
⁵³ *Estado que manifiesta lo que el tribunal de la acordada de Méjico trabajó desde el año de 1703 [sic] en que se cryio, hasta fin del 1809* .... Compiled by Antonio Columna and originally published in the *Registro oficial*, periodico del gobierno, de 11 de octubre de 1830, tom. 3 no. 27, republished in Alamán, *Historia*, Vol. I, append., doc. 1.
⁵⁴ *Recopilación*, lib. 5, tit. 1, ley 1.
⁵⁵ *Instrucciónes*, II, 41.

CHAPTER III

¹ Austin T. Turk, *Criminality and Legal Order* (Chicago, 1969), p. 25.
² *Constitución política de la monarquía Española* (Madrid, 1820), art. 248.
³ *Novísima recopilación de las leyes de España* (Madrid, 1805), lib. 12, tit. 14, ley 3.
⁴ *Ibid.*, ley 4.
⁵ *Recopilación*, lib. 6, tit. 7, ley 12. Other examples are presented in William H. Dusenberry, "Discriminatory Aspects of Legislation in Colonial Mexico," *Journal of Negro History*, XXXIII, 3 (July 1948), 284–302.
⁶ However, those mulattoes, blacks, and coyotes who had distinguished themselves in an acceptable manner were included. *Colección de documentos para la formación social de Hispanoamérica, 1493–1810* (Madrid, 1953–1962), III, 439 (hereafter cited as *Colección*).
⁷ *Instrucciónes*, I, 8.
⁸ *Colección*, III, 825.
⁹ Cornelius de Pauw, the most intemperate proponent of the degeneracy theory, maintained in his work, *Recherches philosophiques sur les Americains* (Berlin, 1768–1769) that the men of the New World, in addition to other alleged evidence of degeneracy, exhibited cowardliness and impotence. For a general review of the issue, see Antonello Gerbi, *La disputa del nuevo mundo* (Mexico, 1960).
¹⁰ Enrique Anderson Imbert, *Spanish-American Literature: A History* (Detroit, 1963), p. 148. The same general theme is followed by Fernández de Lizardi in his most famous work, *El periquillo sarniento* (Mexico, 1816) in which his central character, Periquillo, follows a downward course, including a stay in prison.
¹¹ Quoted in Magnus Mörner, *Race Mixtures in the History of Latin America* (Boston, 1967), p. 59.
¹² *AGN*, Criminal, XXXV, 272–273.
¹³ Delfina E. López Sarrelangue, *Una villa Mexicana en el siglo XVIII* (Mexico, 1957), p. 164.
¹⁴ An individual was often listed as guilty of several types of deviant behavior. Along with a notation of the act that resulted in his arrest were such

vague descriptions as provocative, scandalous, vicious, loose living, prejudicial to the public, and suspected or known to be a habitual criminal. For a typical list, see *AGN*, Presidios y cárceles, IV, 119.

[15] The number released because of lack of evidence is unknown. The acordada listed such cases along with those classified as sufficiently punished without the necessity of a presidio term or other punishment. See appendix.

[16] Turk, *Criminality and Legal Order*, p. 69.

[17] Indians could also appeal acts of corregidores and alcaldes mayores to the juzgado general de indios. C. H. Haring, *The Spanish Empire in America* (New York, 1963), p. 56.

[18] There were some important economic considerations as well. For example a royal decree of 1750 reaffirmed the prohibition against licensing mestizos and mulattoes as scribes or notaries. *Colección*, III, 247. The guilds (gremios) often had restrictions against mixed bloods although in practice, at least by the eighteenth century, they appear to have been ignored. Manuel Carrera Stampa, *Los gremios mexicanos* (Mexico, 1954), p. 226. In addition, the tribute levied against Indians encouraged them to pass for mestizos, who were exempt. Mörner, *Race Mixtures*, p. 69.

[19] Aguirre Beltrán quotes a colonial official to the effect than an overly zealous attempt to determine an individual race or mixture would embarass some well-established families therefore it was wiser to accept a person's declaration. Gonzalo Aguirre Beltrán, *La población negra de Mexico, 1519–1810* (Mexico, 1946), p. 274.

[20] Of the random sampling, the sala processed 400 and the acordada 558 cases. The records generally indicate four racial categories: Spanish, meaning of European origin rather than a native of Spain; mestizo; Indian; and mulatto. A statistically insignificant number of individuals were classified as black, lobos, and coyotes. The figures were taken from documents prepared in 1799 and 1800. Since the actual operation of the acordada changed little between 1756 and the death of Judge Santa María in 1808, they may be taken as overall indicators for that period. *AGN*, Presidios y cárceles, IV, XI, XII.

[21] Carrera Stampa indicates the existence of 200 guilds, many of which involved occupations with extremely minor skills. Consequently, only those tasks that required a well-recognized acquired skill have been classified in the artsisan category while others, although organized, have been placed in the worker category. See appendix.

[22] The fact that members of guilds often held positions on the municipal councils placed them in the middle sector of society. An outstanding example of mestizo upward social mobility is provided by the example of José María Rodalleya, a mestizo and member of the most distinguished and selective guild of silversmiths. Between 1780 and 1812 he served eight times as *veedor* (inspector) of his guild. Carrera Stampa, *Los gremios mexicanos*, p. 226.

[23] The cost of mestizo labor, as well as that of other castes, was less than Spanish labor; consequently, pressure to reduce costs inevitably expanded the opportunities open to them. Ward Barrett, *The Sugar Hacienda of the Marqueses Del Valle* (Minneapolis, 1970), p. 78.

[24] Thorsten Sellin, "Criminology," *Criminal Behavior and Social Systems*, ed. Anthony L. Guenther (Chicago, 1970), p. 10.

[25] William J. Callahan, "The Problem of Confinement: An Aspect of Poor Relief in Eighteenth-Century Spain," *Hispanic American Historical Review*, LI, 1 (February 1971), 9.

[26] Antonio Arbiol, *La familia regulada con doctrina de la sagrada escritura,*

7th ed. (Zaragoza, 1729), quoted in *Hispanic American Historical Review*, LI, 1 (February 1971), 2.

[27] Even Juan Luis Vives urged the poor "not only to support their condition with patience but to embrace it with a will (con gusto) as a don of God." Vives, "Del socorro de los pobres o de las necesidades humanas," *Biblioteca de autores Españoles desde la formación del lenguaje hasta nuestro días* (Madrid, 1922), LXV, 267.

[28] A rough correlation between the price of corn, epidemic disease, and delinquency rates has been established by Enrique Florescano, *Precios del maíz y crisis agrícolas en México (1708–1810)* (Mexico, 1969), p. 169.

[29] The Indians, unable to determine their place in colonial society reacted with resignation interspersed with sudden violence. The drinking problem may also have been a response to social disorientation. Charles Gibson, *The Aztecs Under Spanish Rule* (Stanford, 1964), p. 150. The unstable character of an individual without understandable social guidelines has been studied in a modern setting by William I. Thomas and Florian Znaniecki, *The Polish Peasant in Europe and America*, 2d ed. (New York, 1958).

[30] Garcilaso de la Vega, El Inca, *Royal Commentaries of the Incas and General History of Peru*, trans. Harold V. Livermore (Austin, 1966), I, 607. John Grier Varner, *El Inca, the Life and Times of Garcilaso de la Vega* (Austin, 1968), captures the spirit of the age.

[31] *AGN*, Correspondencia de los virreyes, IV, 25, *Instrucciónes*, II, 41.

[32] *AGN*, Acordada, X, 197.

[33] Alexander von Humboldt, *Political Essay on the Kingdom of New Spain*, 3d ed. (London, 1822), I, 109.

[34] Population estimates have been adapted from D. A. Brading, *Miners and Merchants in Bourbon Mexico 1768–1810* (Cambridge, 1971), p. 14.

[35] In a typical demonstration of zeal and dependability, the acordada responded to viceroy Matías de Gálvez's request for 200 men to put down an Indian revolt in the jurisdiction of Cuayacocotla in 1784 by immediately dispatching 300 men. José Antonio Calderón Quijano, *Los virreyes de Nueva España en el reinado de Carlos III* (Sevilla, 1968), II, 250.

CHAPTER IV

[1] Chevalier notes that at the close of the seventeenth century an unintentional decentralization of authority placed excessive power in the hands of landed proprietors, confronting the central government with the possibility of losing effective control of the viceroyalty. A Mexico City–based and directed acordada obviously strengthened viceregal authority. François Chevalier, *Land and Society in Colonial Mexico* (Berkeley and Los Angeles, 1963), p. 311.

[2] *AGN*, Cédulas, CXXX, 252.

[3] *Recopilación*, lib. 5, tit. 1, ley 1.

[4] *AGN*, Acordada, IV, 259.

[5] An unpaid doctor and pharmacist assisted these officials during Martínez's tenure as judge. *Ibid.*, XXXI, 41.

[6] Service did have limited material rewards; one-third of the value of confiscated property in cases involving prohibited liquors went to the arresting agent while the treasury and the informer shared the remainder. *Ibid.*, IX, 164. In addition, agents did not serve in the militia—an apparently valued

exemption forcing the municipal government of Puebla to request that the number of agents be reduced to release men for service in the provincial regiments of Tlaxcala and Puebla. *Ibid.*, XXV, 206.

[7] Beleña, prov. XI.

[8] Guardhouses were located at Acuhualcingo, Río Frío, Monte de Cruzes, Lupe de Serrano, Cerro Gordo, Perote, Pozuelos, Maltrata, and Aculcingo. *AGN*, Acordada, XXV, 206.

[9] *Ibid.*, XXX, 45.

[10] *Ibid.*, XXXI, 41.

[11] *Ibid.*, III, 59.

[12] One of the earliest manifestations of concern was a cédula dated in 1529. In the eighteenth century, until the tribunal assumed the task of suppression, repeated cédulas proved ineffectual. *Ibid.*, IX, 156.

[13] *Recopilación*, lib. 6, tit. 1, ley 37. Pulque production became a major industry on Spanish haciendas. Charles Gibson, *The Aztecs Under Spanish Rule* (Stanford, 1964), p. 150.

[14] Among many were cane brandy, maguey, mescal, cintincata, odolinque, coco wine, tepache, rabbit's blood, guarapo, and yellow pulque. In a vain effort to keep track of illegal beverages the crown warned the inhabitants not to change or invent new names for the beverages. *AGN*, Acordada, IX, 172.

[15] *Ibid.*, IX, 159.

[16] *Ibid.*, IX, 163.

[17] The ordinance was comprehensive and indicated in detail methods to be employed in the suppression of illegal liquors. Reprinted in 1785, it governed the operations of the juzgado de bebidas prohibidas even after the acordada assumed control. *Ibid.*, IX, 156.

[18] Bucareli noted that only the acordada had sufficient agents and could operate at a very low cost. *Ibid.*, Correspondencia de los virreyes, XXX, 48.

[19] *Ibid.*, XXIV, 51.

[20] *Ibid.*, Acordada, XXII, 533. After the legalization of cane brandy in 1796, there was little justification for the continued existence of the juzgado de bebidas prohibidas. *Ibid.*, Correspondencia de los virreyes, CXCIII, n. 903.

[21] *Ibid.*, Acordada, XXXI, 41.

[22] *Ibid.*, XXX, 159.

[23] *Ibid.*, IX, 193; XXI, 145, 315.

[24] *Ibid.*, Bandos, XIV, 379, art. 83.

[25] *Ibid.*, Acordada, XXIII, 119; VIII, 4, 7.

[26] The regulation required bonded cosigners and loans could not be made for more than three years. *Ibid.*, Bandos, XIV, 379, art. 81.

[27] *Instrucciónes*, II, 47.

[28] Calculated on the basis of two thousand agents at the same salary rate as the lowest paid commissioner (150 pesos annually).

[29] Joaquín Maniau, *Compendio de la historia de la real hacienda de Nueva España* (Mexico, 1914), p. 44.

[30] *AGN*, Acordada, III, 16.

[31] *Ibid.*, XIV, 379.

[32] The regulations advised the treasurer to buy highland maize, rather than that produced in the low coastal areas, even though it might be more expensive, because it was of better quality and produced more flour. Charcoal and firewood were less expensive in the dry season. *Ibid.*, XIV, 379.

[33] *Ibid.*, Acordada, XXXI, 15.

[34] Some confusion exists over the exact relationship of José Velázquez's

legal heir. In correspondence he is referred to both as the son and grandson. Martínez's appointment did not end such pressure, which continued until the death of the heir. The young Velázquez was urged to set up a separate tribunal in Puebla and actually dispensed commissions. That many of Martínez's agents resigned to accept commissions testifies to the continued magic the Velázquez name. Neither the crown nor the viceroy, however, desired a proliferation of separate tribunals and the Puebla acordada was suppressed. *Ibid.*, Cédulas, LXXXVII, esp. 109.

[35] Martínez had suggested Aristimuño as his own replacement. However, Bucareli appointed him only with the idea that if he proved unsatisfactory one of two other candidates Bucareli had investigated would get a turn. *Ibid.*, Correspondencia, LXIV, 30.

[36] Bucareli, writing to José de Gálvez, noted that, "no one better than your excellency understands the importance of this office in New Spain and all that a bad appointment would mean." *Ibid.*, Correspondencia de los virreyes, VC, 13.

[37] Barberi had been an assessor under Aristimuño but was not considered to have the very special talents necessary for the judgeship. Eventually, he found his niche in the junta of revision, as noted in the following chapter.

[38] *Ibid.*, Acordada, IV, 254.

[39] Pedro Martínez de Salazar y Pacheco, "Compendio histórico, político, topografico, hidraulico, económico e instructivo que manifiesta el estado de le jurisdicción de San Juan del Río . . . del año de mil setecientos noventa y tres . . ." *Archivo histórico de hacienda* (colección de documentos publicados bajo la dirección de Jesús Silva Herzog) (Mexico, 1944), III, 149, 162.

[40] *AGN*, Acordada, IX, 322.

[41] *Ibid.*, IX, 192.

[42] *Ibid.*, XI, 151. Although the intendant bore the responsibility to assure that the "Santa Hermandad and its mounted police," complied exactly with its obligations, he could not interfere with the judges privileges. Lillian F. Fisher, *The Intendant System in Spanish America* (Berkeley, 1929), p. 143.

[43] One of the major complaints of the audiencia was the excessive number of these appointments. *AGN*, Acordada, IX, 349.

[44] Then only a small village, Acapulco occasionally experienced the excitement of the arrival of a ship from Peru or Manilla; five agents more than sufficed. In Vera Cruz the situation was not very different. When the fleet arrived the captain-general and several thousand sailors virtually controlled the town; when they left it fell back into its customary tropical torpor. J. H. Parry, *The Spanish Seaborne Empire* (London, 1966), pp. 129–132.

[45] The judge could never be sure exactly how many agents he had at any given moment due to resignations, etc. *AGN*, Acordada, VI, 81.

CHAPTER V

[1] The carrying of small arms by all classes posed a problem. Although the law regulated the manufacture and sale of such items (Recopilación de Castilla, lib. 8, tit. 23, ley 16 and Recopilación de las Indias, lib. 3, tit. 5, ley 12), they were in common use. In 1775 the acordada was charged with their suppression. *AGN*, Correspondencia, XIV, n. 281. Fraud against the tobacco monopoly also became an acordada offense. See Herbert Ingram Priestly,

José de Gálvez, Visitor-General of New Spain (Berkeley, 1916), p. 150. The viceroy also assigned special investigative functions to the tribunal. One such assignment led to the breaking up of a contraband ring in Tampico and Panuco which involved royal officials. *AGN*, Correspondencia, LXXXIV, n. 2537; LXXXVI, n. 2691.

2 The distinction between jurisdictions was clearly stated, "as agents of the hermandad they must pursue some, as dependents of the acordada others and as ministers of the juzgado privativo [de bebidas prohibidas] others." *AGN*, Acordada, IX, 181.

3 The regulations defined villages or rural areas as having less than thirty inhabitants. *Ibid.*, IX, 182.

4 *Ibid.*, Bandos, IX, 56; *ibid.*, Acordada, IX, 182.

5 The only legal exception involved the clergy. In cases involving individuals subject to the ecclesiastical fuero the agent cooperated with the ecclesiastical judge and left sentencing in his hands. *Ibid.*, IX, 163.

6 Indians were never specifically deprived of this privilege, an omission that caused some dispute. *Ibid.*, Correspondencia, IV, exp. 465; *ibid.*, Acordada, XXIV, 312.

7 The use of church asylum had long been a matter of concern. The fuero real had exempted certain classes of crimes and in 1737 a concordat with the papacy further restricted their use by declaring certain churches to be *iglesias frías* which could not offer asylum. *Novísima recopilación de las leyes de España*, lib. 1, tit. 4, ley 4. In Mexico widespread use of churches by criminals had a detrimental effect on order and in some cases endangered the life of the clergy and the faithful. In 1774 the diocese of Mexico limited asylum in Mexico City to the parish churches of San Miguel and Santa Catalina while outside the capital the principal parish church, those of the regular clergy, and churches more than four leagues from a church sanctuary could be used. Included in the area of the church was the cemetery, presumably to avoid overcrowding of the building itself. *Biblioteca nacional, MS.* 350 (1377).

8 Alamán noted that a cédula of December 21, 1765, provided for a verbal sentencing in the presence of the judge, two assessors, and a defensor (Lucas Alamán, *Historia de Méjico* [Mexico, 1849], 1, 55); however, the correct date of the cédula is December 21, 1756. *AGN*, Acordada, XXX, 45.

9 The assessor general of the viceroyalty called the regulations a glorious monument to the zeal and rectitude of the justice of Aristimuño. *Ibid.*, IX, 193.

10 The regulation noted that it was better for the guilty to escape punishment than be forced to confess. *Ibid.*, IX, 184.

11 In the total absence of other witnesses they could give evidence, excluding only a declared enemy. *Ibid.*

12 In addition, agents exercised their judgment by supplying any other pertinent documentation. *Ibid.*, IX, 186.

13 *Ibid.*, IX, 321. Probably as a consequence of the isolation, many prisoners appeared unaware of the exact reason for their imprisonment or the state of the case, and were forced to live in uncertainty until suddenly sentenced. *Ibid.*, XVII, 49.

14 Whether apprehended by the tribunal or by ordinary judicial authorities, all prisoners guilty of violating liquor laws were exempt from regular prison inspections without the special permission of the arresting officer. *Ibid.*,

IX, 165. Ordinary justices could also conduct such searches without permission. Ibid., IX, 166.

[15] Ibid., IX, 178.

[16] Ibid., Correspondencia, CVIII, 50.

[17] Ibid., Acordada, IV, 261.

[18] Ibid., XXX, 159.

[19] Ibid., X, 198.

[20] Laws governing the operation of prisons did not specifically exclude the tribunal. Recopilación, lib. 7, tit. 6.

[21] AGN, Acordada, X, 159. At the beginning of the nineteenth century, Baron von Humboldt described the tribunal's prison as spacious, well aired, and suited for its purpose. Alexander von Humboldt, Political Essay on the Kingdom of New Spain (London, 1822), II, 38.

[22] Charles Gibson, The Aztecs Under Spanish Rule (Stanford, 1964), p. 150.

[23] See appendix. During epidemics prisoners helped clean the city's canals in an effort to reduce the spread of disease. Donald B. Cooper, Epidemic Disease in Mexico City, 1761-1813 (Austin, 1965), p. 19.

[24] Richard E. Greenleaf, "The Obraje in the Late Mexican Colony," The Americas, XXIII, 3 (January 1967), 242.

[25] José Miranda noted that obraje sentences were abolished in the latter part of the century; see Alfonso Caso et al., Métodos y resultados de la política indigenista en México (Mexico, 1954), p. 67.

[26] For an interesting discussion of crown policy toward hostile Indians, see Christon I. Archer, "The Deportation of Barbarian Indians From the Internal Provinces of New Spain, 1789-1810," The Americas, XXIX (January 1973), 376-385.

[27] A royal decree of September 21, 1726, ordered that "legitimate and actual" Spaniards be exempt from workhouse (obraje) confinement. Colección, III, 189. By the late eighteenth century such restrictions had become meaningless.

[28] For example, the governor of Acapulco requested an additional one hundred prisoners to assist in repairing storm damage, noting that the fifty already at work had saved the adminstration a considerable sum of money over the estimated expense of hired labor. AGN, Presidios y cárceles, XII, 168.

[29] Another explanation for leniency may have been the fact that the viceroy, with the advice of the sala del crimen, sentenced all prisoners removed from asylum. Alicia Bazán Alarcón, "El real tribunal de la Acordada y la delincuencia en la Nueva España," Historia Mexicana, XIII, 3 (Enero-Marzo, 1964), 329. Prisoners sentenced to ship service but found to be unfit were sent to presidios for a period equal to one-half the original sentence. Novísima recopilación de las leyes de España (Madrid, 1805), lib. 12, tit. 40, ley 16.

[30] Not surprisingly few slaves were processed by judicial authorities. Owner preferred to sell unruly individuals rather than lose their investment and the labor of their slave.

[31] A pragmática of March 12, 1771 placed such limitations on sentence to places of confinement in Spain and a royal order of August 24, 1772, lowered the maximum to six years in Puerto Rico, Cartagena de Indias, and Havana. Novísima recopilación de las leyes de España (Madrid, 1805), lib. 12, tit. 40, ley 7 and 15.

[32] AGN, Cédulas, CXXXIV, 164.

[33] Ibid., Criminal, LVIII, 179.

34 *Ibid.*, LVIII, 187.
35 *Ibid.*, Cédulas, CXLVIII, 37.
36 *Ibid.*, Acordada, IX, 314.
37 In order to make the suggestion more acceptable to the acordada the members of the new body would be drawn from the audiencias of Santo Domingo, Caracas, Guatemala, Manila, and Guadalajara. *Ibid.*, IX, 349.
38 *Ibid.*, Cédulas, CXLVIII, 37.
39 In 1793 the junta received 638 cases with a total of 20,127 pages of testimony. *Ibid.*, Acordada, IX, 471.
40 Barberi was not one of the original members but a replacement for a member who resigned shortly after the establishment of the junta to accept a post in Durango, *Ibid.*, Cédulas, CLXIII, 165. He had served as an assessor under Santa María who removed him from that office alleging that he did not perform his duties in a satisfactory manner. José Antonio Calderón Quijano, *Los virreyes de Nueva España en el reinado de Carlos III* (Sevilla, 1968), II, 250.
41 *AGN*, Acordada, XXII, 474.
42 *Ibid.*, Cédulas, CLXXXVI, 39.
43 In 1790 the tribunal processed 2,464 cases; in 1791, 2,010; 1792, 2,119. The year previous to the junta's establishment the number totaled 2,219. The year 1788 was in fact the lean year with only 1,853 cases processed. *Ibid.*, Acordada, X, 197.
44 Viceregal authorities constantly worried over local resistance to the tribunal fearing that it would destroy the organization's usefulness. Repeated bandos warned provincial officers to preserve its dignity and authority.

CHAPTER VI

1 *AGN*, Acordada, XXXI, 26.
2 José Antonio Calderón Quijano, *Los virreyes de Nueva España en el reinado de Carlos III* (Sevilla, 1968), II, 314.
3 *AGN*, Cédulas, XLIV, 98.
4 *Ibid.*, I, 46.
5 José Manuel de Castro Santa Anna, *Diario de sucesos notables* (Documentos para la historia de Méjico, vols. IV and V) (Mexico, 1854), IV, 139, 169.
6 *AGN*, Cédulas, LXV, 70.
7 Fernando Casado Fernández-Mensaque, "El tribunal de la acordada de Nueva España," *Anuario de estudios Americanos*, XVIII (1950), 32.
8 *AGN*, Correspondencia, LXIX, 32.
9 *Ibid.*, XIV, 310.
10 *Ibid.*, Cédulas, CXXI, 312.
11 *Ibid.*, Acordada, VI, 37.
12 *Ibid.*, XVII, 330.
13 *Ibid.*, XII 347.
14 *Ibid.*, XVIII, 252.
15 *Ibid.*, VI, 337.
16 *Instrucciónes*, I, 116.
17 *AGN*, Acordada, XXII, 76.
18 *Ibid.*, Cédulas, CLXVI, 52.
19 *Ibid.*, Acordada, XVI, 307.

20 *Ibid.*, VII, 8.
21 *Ibid.*, XII, 1.
22 *Ibid.*, XXVII, 166.
23 *Ibid.*, VI, 276.
24 The viceroy attempted to end this problem by ruling that an agent need only present his commission on appointment; recognition of it was to be kept on file so that in the event of a change in local officials they would be aware of such a commission. *Ibid.*, Bandos, V, 53.
25 *Ibid.*, Acordada, XIV, 284.
26 *Ibid.*, XIV, 314. Only the transfer of prisoners from Mexico City to presidios to serve sentences was at the expense of the viceregal treasury. *Mercedes y pensiones limosnas y salarios en la real hacienda de la Nueva España* (Archivo histórico de hacienda, colección de documentos publicados bajo la dirección de Jesús Silva Herzog) (Mexico, 1945), V, 156.
27 AGN, Acordada, XVIII, 10.
28 *Ibid.*, XXV, 14.
29 *Ibid.*, Bandos, VI, 41.
30 *Ibid.*, Acordada, XXIII, 55.
31 *Ibid.*, VII, 66.
32 Lyle N. McAlister, *The "Fuero Militar" in New Spain 1764-1800* (Gainesville, 1957), p. 14.
33 AGN, Acordada, VII, 13.
34 *Ibid.*, VII, 292.
35 McAlister, *"Fuero Militar,"* p. 80.
36 *Instrucciónes*, I, 325.
37 *Ibid.*, 110.
38 AGN, Bandos, XIII, 64.
39 *Instrucciónes*, II, 41.
40 AGN, Acordada, IV, 261.
41 *Ibid.*, IV, 318.
42 *Ibid.*, IX, 196.
43 *Ibid.*, XVII, 70; IV, 392.

CHAPTER VII

1 AGN, Acordada, IX, 320.
2 Alexander von Humboldt, *Political Essay on the Kingdom of New Spain* (London, 1822), II, 6.
3 AGN, Acordada, XXVI, 357.
4 *Ibid.*, Correspondencia, CLVIII, 182.
5 Joaquín Maniau, *Compendio de la historia de la real hacienda de Nueva España* (Mexico, 1914), p. 72.
6 AGN, Correspondencia, CLXXXIII, 903.
7 *Ibid.*, Acordada, VII, 453.
8 *Ibid.*, XXI, 7.
9 *Ibid.*, Correspondencia, CCL, 35.
10 *Ibid.*, Acordada, XXII, 533.
11 *Ibid.*, XXVIII, 322.
12 *Ibid.*, Correspondencia, CXXXIII, 422.
13 *Ibid.*, Acordada, XXII, 465.
14 Constitución, arts, 246, 298, and 300.

[15] The constitution of 1812 eliminated a number of special jurisdictions including the relatively innocuous *mesta*. William H. Dusenberry, *The Mexican Mesta: The Administration of Ranching in Colonial Mexico* (Urbana, 1963), p. 192.

[16] En los negocios comúnes, civiles y criminales no habra más que un solo fuero para toda clase de personas. *Constitución*, art. 248.

[17] *AGN*, Acordada, XXII, 471. The tribunal ceased operations on May 31, 1813.

[18] *Ibid.*, X, 458.

CONCLUSION

[1] Paul Vanderwood, "Genesis of the Rurales: Mexico's Early Struggle for Public Security," *Hispanic American Historical Review*, L, 2 (May 1970), p. 323.

WORKS CITED

Sources for AGN references were at the Archivo General de la Nación, Mexico City in the following sections:
Acordada
Bandos y ordenanazas
Correspondencia de los virreyes
Criminal
Presidios y cárceles
Real cédulas

Aguirre Beltrán, Gonzalo. *La población negra de México, 1519–1810.* Mexico, 1946.
——. "El gobierno indígena en México y el proceso de aculturación," *América Indígena,* XII, 4 (October 1952), 271–297.
Alamán, Lucas. *Historia de Méjico.* 5 vols. Mexico, 1849.
Amador, Elias. *Bosquejo histórico de Zacatecas.* Zacatecas, 1892.
Anderson Imbert, Enrique. *Spanish-American Literature: A History.* Detroit, 1963.
Archer, Christon I. "The Deportation of Barbarian Indians From the Internal Provinces of New Spain, 1789–1810," *The Americas,* XXIX (January 1973), 376–385.
Bancroft, Hubert Howe. *History of Mexico.* 6 vols. San Francisco, 1886–1888.
Barrett, Ward J. *The Sugar Hacienda of the Marqueses Del Valle.* Minneapolis, 1970.
Bazán Alarcón, Alicia. "El Real Tribunal de la Acordada y La Delincuencia en La Nueva España," *Historia Mexicana,* XIII, 3 (Enero-Marzo 1964), 317–345 (originally written as Master's thesis, Universidad Nacional Autonoma de Mexico, Mexico, 1963).
Beleña, Eusebio Ventura. *Recopilación sumaria de todos los autos acordadas de la real audiencia y sala del crimen de Nueva España.* Mexico, 1787.
Borah, Woodrow. *New Spain's Century of Depression.* Berkeley and Los Angeles, 1951.
——. "Social Welfare and Social Obligation in New Spain: A Tentative Assessment," XXXVI Congreso Internacional de Americanistas, *Actas y Memorias,* IV (1966), 45–57.
Brading, D. A. *Miners and Merchants in Bourbon Mexico 1763–1810.* Cambridge, 1971.
Calderón Quijano, José Antonio. *Los virreys de Nueva España en el reinado de Carlos III.* 2 vols. Sevilla, 1968.

Callahan, William J. "The Problem of Confinement: An Aspect of Poor Relief in Eighteenth-Century Spain," *Hispanic American Historical Review*, LI, 1 (February 1971), 1–24.

Carrera Stampa, Manuel. *Los gremios Mexicanos*. Mexico, 1954.

Carrión Antonio. *Historia de la cuidad de la Puebla de Los Angeles*. 2 vols. Puebla, 1896.

Caso, Alfonso. *Métodos y resultados de la política indigenista en México*. Mexico, 1954.

Castro Santa-Anna, José Manuel de. *Diario de sucesos notables*. 3 vols. Mexico, 1854. Documentos para la historia de Méjico, ser. 1, IV–VI.

Chamberlain, Robert S. "The Concept of the Señor Natural as Revealed by Castilian Law and Administrative Documents," *Hispanic American Historical Review*, XIX, 2 (May 1939), 130–137.

Chávez Orozco, Luis. *Las instituciónes democráticas de los indígenas mexicanos en la época colonial*. Mexico, 1942.

Chevalier, François. *Land and Society in Colonial Mexico: The Great Hacienda*. Berkeley and Los Angeles, 1963.

Colección de documentos para la formación social de Hispanoamérica, 1493–1810. 3 vols. Madrid, 1953–1962.

Constitución política de la monaquía Española. Madrid, 1820.

Cooper, Donald B. *Epidemic Disease in Mexico City, 1761–1813*. Austin, 1965.

Díaz, Bernal. *Historia verdadera de la conquista de la Nueva España*. 5th ed. Mexico, 1960.

Dusenberry, William H. "Discriminatory Aspects of Legislation in Colonial Mexico," *Journal of Negro History*, XXXIII, 3 (July 1948), 284–302.

———. *The Mexican Mesta: The Administration of Ranching in Colonial Mexico*. Urbana, 1963.

Elliot, J. H. *Imperial Spain, 1464–1716*. London, 1963.

Escobar, Fr. Diego Antonio de. *Sermón epedictio . . . hizo el día 22 de Septiembre de este año de 1732 . . . al Cap pⁿ D. Miguel Velázquez Lorea. . . .* Mexico, 1732.

Fisher, Lillian F. *The Intendant System in Spanish America*. Berkeley, 1929.

Florescano, Enrique. *Precios del maíz y crisis agrícolas en México 1708–1810*. Mexico. 1969.

Garcilaso de la Vega, El Inca. *Royal Commentaries of the Incas and General History of Peru*. Trans. Harold V. Livermore. Austin, 1966. 1966.

Gemelli Carreri, Juan Francisco. *Las cosas más considerables en la Nueva España*. Trans. José María de Agreda y Sanchez. Mexico, 1946.

Gerbi, Antonello. *La disputa del nuevo mundo*. Mexico, 1960.

Gibson, Charles. *The Aztecs Under Spanish Rule*. Stanford, 1964.

Gómara, Francisco López de. *Cortés: The Life of the Conqueror by His Secretary*. Trans. Lesley Byrd Simpson. Berkeley and Los Angeles, 1965.

González Obregón, Luis. *Rebeliónes indígenas y precursores de la independencia mexicana en los siglos XVI, XVII y XVIII*. 2d ed. rev. Mexico, 1952.
Goubert, Paul, S. J. "Byzance et l'Espagne wisigothique (554–711)," *Études Byzantines*. II (1944), 5–78.
Greenleaf, Richard E. "The Obraje in the Late Mexican Colony," *The Americas*, XXIII, 3 (January 1967), 227–250.
Guthrie, Chester Lyle. "Colonial Economy, Trade, Industry and Labor in Seventeenth Century Mexico City," *Revista de historia de América*, no. 7 (1939), pp. 103–134.
———. "Riots in Seventeenth Century Mexico City: A Study of Social and Economic Conditions," *Greater America, Essays in Honor of Herbert Eugene Bolton*. Berkeley and Los Angeles, 1945. Pp. 243–258.
Hamnett, Brian R. *Politics and Trade in Southern Mexico*. Cambridge, 1971.
Haring, C. H. *The Spanish Empire in America*. New York, 1963.
Humboldt, Alexander von. *Political Essay on the Kingdom of New Spain*. 3 vols. London, 1822.
Instrucciónes que los virreys de Nueva España dejaron a sus sucesores. 2 vols. Mexico, 1867–1873.
Jones, A. H. M. *Studies in Roman Government and Law*. Oxford, 1960.
Karst, Kenneth L. *Latin American Legal Institutions: Problems for Comparative Study*. Berkeley and Los Angeles, 1966.
Lee, Raymond L. "Grain Legislation in Colonial Mexico, 1575–1585," *Hispanic American Historical Review*, XXVII, 4 (November 1947), 647–660.
Lobingier, Charles Sumner. "Las Siete Partidas and Its Predecessors," *California Law Review*, I (1913), 487–498.
López Sarrelangue, Delfina E. *Una villa Mexicana en el siglo XVIII*. Mexico, 1957.
Los códigos Españoles concordados y anotados. 12 vols. Madrid, 1847–1851.
Lunenfeld, Marvin. *The Council of the Santa Hermandad: A Study of the Pacification Forces of Ferdinand and Isabella*. Coral Gables, 1970.
McAlister, Lyle N. *The "Fuero Militar" in New Spain 1764–1800*. Gainesville, 1957.
———. "Social Structure and Social Change in New Spain," *Hispanic American Historical Review*, XLIII, 3 (August 1963), 349–370.
Maniau, Joaquín. *Compendio de la historia de la real hacienda de Nueva España*. Mexico, 1914.
Martin, Norman F. *Los vagabundos en la Nueva España, siglo XVI*. Mexico, 1957.
Mensaque, Fernando Casado Fernández. "El tribunal de la acordada de Nueva España," *Anuario de estudios Americanos*, XVIII (1950), 279–323.
Mercedes y pensiones, limosnas y salarios en la real hacienda de la Nu-

eva España. Archivo histórico de hacienda. Colección de documentos publicados bajo la dirección de Jésus Silva Herzog, V. Mexico, 1945.

Merriman, Roger Bigelow. *The Rise of the Spanish Empire in the Old World and the New.* 4 vols. New York, 1962.

Monteiros, Fr. Ignacio Espinoza de los. *Oración continua funebre ... hizo el día 17 de Mayo de este año de 1756 ... al Joseph Velázquez Lorea.* ... Mexico, 1756.

Moore, John Preston. *The Cabildo in Peru Under the Hapsburgs.* Durham, 1954.

Mörner, Magnus. *Race Mixtures in the History of Latin America.* Boston, 1967.

Morse, Richard M. "Some Characteristics of Latin American Urban History," *American Historical Review,* LXVII, 2 (January 1962), 317–338.

Muro Orejón, Antonio. "Leyes del nuevo código de Indias vigentes en América," *Revista de Indias,* V, 17 (July–September 1944), 433–472.

Novísima recopilación de las leyes de España. 6 vols. Madrid, 1805–1829.

O'Gorman, Edmundo. *The Invention of America.* Bloomington, Ind., 1961.

Orozco y Berra, Manuel. *Noticia histórica de la conjuración del Marqués del Valle. Años 1565–1568.* Mexico, 1853.

Ots Capdequi, José María. *España en América; las instituciónes coloniales.* 2d ed. Bogota, 1952.

———. *Instituciónes.* Barcelona, 1959.

———. "Las fuentes del derecho indiano," *Humanidades,* Vol. XXV, hist. part. 1 (1936), pp. 23–36.

Padden, R. C. *The Hummingbird and the Hawk.* New York, 1970.

Panes y Abellán, Diego. *Cronología de los virreys que han gobernado esta Nueva España desde el invicto conquistador D. Fernando Cortés, hasta el que al presente gobierno; con noticias particulares de sucesos acaecidos en sus tiempos.* Mexico, n.d.

Parry, J. H. *The Audiencia of New Galicia in the Sixteenth Century.* Cambridge, 1968.

———. *The Spanish Seaborne Empire.* London, 1966.

———. *The Spanish Theory of Empire in the Sixteenth Century.* Cambridge, 1940.

Phelan, John Leddy. *The Kingdom of Quito in the Seventeenth Century.* Madison, 1967.

Portillo y Weber, José López. *La rebelión de Nueva Galicia.* Mexico, 1939.

Priestley, Herbert Ingram. *José de Gálvez, Visitor-General of New Spain.* Berkeley, 1916.

———. *The Mexican Nation, A History.* New York, 1923.

Puyol y Alonso, Julio. *Las hermandades de Castilla y León.* Madrid, 1913.

Recopilación de leyes de los reynos de las Indias. Madrid, 1791.
Robles, Antonio de. *Diario de sucesos notables (1665–1703)*. Antonio Castro Leal, ed. 3 vols. Mexico, 1946.
Romero Flores, Jesús. *México–historia de una gran ciudad*. Mexico, 1953.
Salazar y Pacheco, Martínez de. "Compendio histórico, político, topografico, hidraulico, económico, e instructivo que manifiesta el estado de San Juan del Río de la provincia de México," *Archivo histórico de hacienda*. Colección de documentos publicados bajo la dirección de Jesús Silva Herzog (1944) III, 141–185.
Sauer, Carl Ortwin. *The Early Spanish Main*. Berkeley and Los Angeles, 1969.
Scott, S. P. *History of the Moorish Empire in Europe*. 3 vols. Philadelphia, 1904.
Sedaño, Francisco. *Noticias de México*. 2 vols. Mexico, 1880.
Sellin, Thorsten. "Criminology," *Criminal Behavior and Social Systems*. Ed. Anthony L. Guenther. Chicago, 1970.
Sigüenza y Góngora, Carlos. *Alboroto y motín do los indios de México del 8 de junio de 1692*. Ed. Irving A. Leonard. Mexico, 1932.
Simpson, Lesley Byrd. *The Encomienda in New Spain*. Berkeley and Los Angeles, 1950.
Solórzano Pereira, Juan. *Política indiana*. Madrid, 1736.
Soustelle, Jacques. *The Daily Life of the Aztecs on the Eve of the Spanish Conquest*. Stanford, 1970.
Thomas, William I., and Florian Znaniecki. *The Polish Peasant in Europe and America*. 2d ed. 2 vols. New York, 1958.
Thompson, E. A. *The Goths in Spain*. Oxford, 1969.
Thompson, Eric S., ed. *Thomas Gage's Travels in the New World*. Norman, Okla., 1958.
Turk, Austin T. *Criminality and Legal Order*. Chicago, 1969.
Valle-Arispe, Artemio de. *Historia de la ciudad de México, según los relatos de sus cronistas*. 4th ed. Mexico, 1946.
Vanderwood, Paul. "Genesis of the Rurales: Mexico's Early Struggle for Public Security," *Hispanic American Historical Review*, L, 2 (May 1970), 323–344.
Van Kleffens, E. N. *Hispanic Law Until the End of the Middle Ages*. Edinburgh, 1968.
Varner, John Grier. *El Inca, the Life and Times of Garcilasco de la Vega*. Austin, 1968.
Velasco y Mendoza, Luis. *Historia de la cuidad de Celaya*. 3 vols. Mexico, 1947.
Vives, Juan Luis. "Del socorro de los pobres o de las necesidades humanas," *Biblioteca de autores Españoles desde la formación del lenguaje hasta nuestro días*. Vol. LXV. Madrid, 1922.
Walton, Clifford Stevens. *The Civil Law in Spain and Spanish America*. Washington, D.C., 1900.

INDEX

Acapulco, 67, 81
Acordada agents: territorial jurisdiction of, 54; salaried, 58–59; administrative, 60–61; commissions and ranks of, 65; distribution of, 66–67; selection of, 66; number of, 67; in urban areas, 70; professionalism of, 74; limitation of proposed, 83; and military privileges, 105
Acordada prison: general warning at entrance to, 34; operations of, 62; procedures of, 72; inspection of, 77–78
Alcalde mayor, 24, 41
Alcaldes de cortes, 9
Alcaldes del crimen. *See* Sala del crimen
Alfonso X (el sabio), 6, 7, 9
Appeals: in case of illegal liquors, 76; to viceroy, 81–82; advocated by audiencia, 83
Aristimuño, Francisco Antonio: handles backlog of cases, 56; as a lieutenant, 58; and reglamento, 72; and conflict with sala del crimen, 93
Audiencia: under Henry II, 9; reorganization of in 1433, 9; location of, 12; in New World, 13; early activities of, 17; and Martín Cortés, 20; in New Spain, 21–23; operations up to 1695, 23; proposes to limit acordada, 83; honorary appointment of acordada judge to, 89; of Guadalajara attempts to establish its own acordada, 95

Banditry: growth of, 28; disruption by of commerce and communication, 31; Miguel Velázquez controls, 33; José Velázquez controls, 33–34; as a challenge to the state, 42; activities of guarda major de caminos against, 55, 69–70; capital punishment for, 79
Baratillo (thieves market), 31
Barberi, José: as interim judge, 64; on junta de revisión, 85
Branciforte, Marqués de: ends jurisdictional limitations on agents, 101
Bucareli, Antonio María: defends acordada, 92, 99
Buena Vista, 105

Caciques: in a European framework, 15; movement of toward a nonhereditary officialdom, 25; considered under laws, 38; punishment of, 76, 81
Capitulación (of Santa Fe), 12
Chancillerías, 12
Cholula, 96
Church: as sanctuary, 70–71; punishment of those removed from, 81
Classes: crown interest in supporting relative position of, 38; attitude of authorities toward lower, 39, 43; of agents, 65
Columna, Antonio: appointed judge, 104; organizes road guard, 105; travels to Spain, 105
Concha, Martínez de la: appointed judge of acordada, 55; background of, 64; reorganization under, 71–72; number of illegal liquor cases handled by, 77; membership of in audiencia, 89
Constitutio Antoniniana (A.D. 212), 4
Constitution of 1812: and operation

of the acordada, 106; as applied to criminal justice, 106-107
Consulado of Cádiz, 57; financial support of, 58
Córdova, 66, 77, 96
Corregidores: under Alfonso XI (1312-1350), 10; introduction of, in Mexico, 17; subordination of, in judicial functions, 23
Cortés, Hernán: relationship of with the crown, 13; and Indian society, 14
Cortés, Martín, conspiracy of, 19-20
Council of the Indies, 39
Creoles, attitude of colonial society toward, 39-40
Crime: motivation of, 47-50; prevalence of, 50-51; under jurisdiction of hermandad, 69; under jurisdiction of guarda mayor de caminos, 69-70; types and frequency of, 78-79; punishment for, 81; covered by pardons, 82
Cuarteles, 24-25
Cuautla, 97
Cuernavaca, 67, 100

Debt: private imprisonment for abolished, 11; pardons given for, 82

Encomienda: establishment of under Cortés, 16; attempt to reduce, 17-19

Flores, Juan José, last judge, 105
Fortescue, Sir John, 48
Freud, Sigmund, 49
Fuero, Juzgo, 5, 7
Fuero Real (1255), 6, 7, 8

Gálvez, Matías de: inspects acordada prison, 77-78; attitude of toward acordada, 99
Garcilaso de la Vega, the Inca: example of defective self-concepts, 49-50
Guadalajara, 30, 35, 66, 77, 103
Guanajuato, 67
Guarda de pito, 24
Guarda mayor de caminos: joined with acordada, 55; criminal acts under jurisdiction of, 69-70; atrophied, 102; interim appointment of Antonio Columna to, 104

Havana, 81
Henry II (1369-1379), 9
Hermandad: historical development of, 10; authority of after reorganization by Isabella, 11; established in New Spain, 26; becomes core of acordada, 32; criminal acts under jurisdiction of, 69; exempt from authority of sala del crimen, 70; attempt by sala to limit acordada authority to, 92; at beginning of nineteenth century, 102
Humboldt, Baron Alexander von, 51, 102

Indians: as a class subject to presidio sentences, 46; crime of in ratio to population, 52; and hermandad, 70; punishment of for illegal liquors, 76; sentenced to presidios, 80; used to conduct prisoners, 97
Indian society: and Spanish political theory, 15; required to adopt municipal structure, 25; disruption of, 26; Spanish attitudes toward, 30, 47; inability of to conform to Spanish norms, 40; acceptance by of paternalistic law enforcement, 42
Intendant, 66, 95
Investigative methods, 73

Juárez, Benito, 111
Junta de revisión: establishment and composition of, 84; effects of, 85; handling by of cases, 86; as evidence of viceregal concern, 110
Junta de seguridad y buen orden, 105
Jurisdictional conflicts: attitude of sala del crimen toward, 89; opposition of audiencia of Guadalajara in, 89, 94; sala del crimen attempts to limit, 92; over carrying small arms, 93; over acordada's right to try dependents, 93; with local officials, 96-97; with military, 98-99
Justinian, 5

Index

Juzgado de bebidas prohibidas: placed under acordada, 57; importance of, 58; authority of, 70; procedures of, 75–76; and distribution of agents, 77; number of cases under, 77; violation of military of, 98–99; at beginning of nineteenth century, 103; interim appointment of Antonio Columna to, 104; sala del crimen urges separation of, 105
Juzgado general de Indios, 25

Laws of Burgos, 2
Laws of Toro (1505), 3, 12
Lex Romana Visigothorum, 5
Linares, Duke of, 32
Lizardi, José Joaquín Fernández de: portrays the creole character, 39–40

Marquesado del Valle, authority of the acordada in, 54
Marqués de Croix, prohibits sale of convicts by acordada, 56
Marqués de Cruillos, concerned over methods used by agents, 55
Mescal, revenue from, 103
Mestizos: impact of growing numbers of, 26; and demand for labor, 28; attitude of judicial authorities toward, 41; presidio sentences given to, 45; subverted self-concept by as motivation to crime, 49; ratio of to criminal cases, 52; sentenced to overseas presidios, 80; supplementary punishment of, 81
Military service, 76, 81; Indians exempted from, 80
Mixton war (1541), 18
Moors: impact of on the laws, 5; disruption by of legal unification, 6; acordada prisoners compared to captives of, 34
Mulattoes: Bartolomé de Góngora portrays, 41; presidio sentences given to, 46; ratio of to criminal cases, 52; sentenced to overseas presidios, 80, supplementary punishment of, 81
Municipal magistrates: territorial limitations of, 24; approach to enforcement, 24; connection of with hermandad, 27; attitude toward illegal liquors, 76; conflict with acordada, 96–97

New Galicia, 95, 97
New Laws of 1542, 18–19
Novísima recopilación de leyes de España (1805), 12, 37
Nueva recopilación de Castilla (1569), 3, 12
Nuevo código de leyes de Indios (1792), 3
Nuño de Guzmán, Beltrán, 17

Oaxaca, 103
Obrajes: convict labor of, 27; for violation of liquor laws, 76; price of, 80
Occupation: as indicator of class, 44; of presidio prisoners, 44–47; of agents, 65
Ordenamiento de Alcalá de Henares (1348), 8
Ordenanzas Reales (1484), 12
Ordinance of the Cortes de Zamora, 9
Otumba, 97, 105

Pardons: nature of, 82; category of crimes covered by, 82
Pátzquaro, 97
Pax porfiriana, 112
Pensacola, 81
Philippines, 81, 90
Physiognomics, 47
Piedras Negras, 81
Porta, Giambattista della, 47
Presidios: race and classes subject to imprisonment in, 44–47; as most important form of punishment, 80; location of, 81; length of sentence to, 81; escapees from, 94
Prisoners: number of processed, 34, 51; volume of handled by acordada, 36; maintenance of, 58; treatment of, 73; indefinite custody of, 75; in acordada prison, 77–78; age and physical condition of considered, 80; as property of processing agency, 94; disputes over local assistance for, 96–97

Provincias internas, 103
Puebla, 66, 67, 83, 96, 98, 102, 103, 105
Pulque: as a source of revenue, 56, 57; rise in revenue of, 77
Punishment: noted by diarists 28–29; after riot of 1692, 30; unequal application of, 37–38; paternalistic imposition of, 42; in presidios, 44–47; for illegal liquors, 76, capital, 79; and presidio confinement, 80, 81; other methods of, 81; depersonalization of, 109–110

Queen Isabella, and use of hermandad, 10
Querétaro, 32, 66, 77

Race: as source of conflict in riot of 1692, 29; in relation to percent of criminal cases, 52
Recopilación de leyes de los Reynos de las Indias: completeness of, 3; sets order of application, 3; position of caciques in, 38
Reglamento of 1775 and 1776: practices incorporated into, 72; procedure under, 72–73; exception to, 74
Residencia, exemption of acordada judges from, 89
Revilla Gigedo, Conde de (the elder), attitude toward José Velázquez, 99
Revilla Gigedo, Conde de (the younger): authorizes regulation of juzgado de bebidas prohibidas, 75; attitude of toward acordada, 99; puts limits on agents, 100
Riots: of 1624, 28; of 1692, 29; concern over, 48
Roman law: nature of, 4; modification under Visigoths, 5; revival of study, 7
Royal justice: informal development of, 8; institutionalization of under Ordinance of the Cortes de Zamora, 9
Rurales, 111, 112

Sala de crimen: as part of audiencia, 21–22; status of, 23; appears unable to contain banditry. 31; and authority over acordada, 70; complains about methods of acordada, 71; proposes to supervise appointments, 83; members of or junta de revisión, 86; jurisdictional conflict of, 89; requests same powers as acordada, 91; contests viceroy's power to appoint acordada judge, 92; opposes attempt by acordada to claim jurisdiction over agents, 94; proprietary attitude of toward prisoners, 94; urges separation of juzgado de bebidas prohibidas, 105; advises splitting of acordada, 106
San Juan del Río, 65
San Luis de la Paz, 96
Santa María, Manuel Antonio de: recorded in song, 34; number of illegal liquor cases handled by, 77; capital punishment imposed by, 79; attitude of toward junta de revisión, 85–86; presses for small arms privileges, 93; attempts to try own dependents, 94; and conflict with military over liquor regulations, 98; defends unlimited jurisdiction, 100–101; surveys guardhouses, 103; death and replacement of, 104
Siete Partidas (1265), 7, 8
Slaves, presidio punishment of, 81
Spaniards: as vagabonds, 26; number of sentenced to presidios, 44; ratio of to criminal cases, 52; punishment of in liquors cases, 76; sentenced to overseas presidios, 80
Spanish law: application of in the Indies, 3; development of, 3–8; order of under the Ordenamiento de Alcalá de Henares, 8; amorphous quality of, 14
Subdelegados, attitudes of toward Indians, 41

Tacuba, 67
Tejada, Sebastián Lerdo de, 111
Texcoco, 67
Tlaxcala, 30
Tobacco monopoly: right to carry small arms, 93

Toluca, 67, 105
Tula, 67

Vagrancy: of Spaniards, 26; as feature of colonial life, 31; punishment for, 31
Valero, Marqués de, 32
Valiente, Pedro de, and violation of liquor laws, 98
Velázquez, José: becomes judge, 33; organizes procedures, 55; suppresses illegal liquors, 56; proprietary rights of, 63; and membership in audiencia, 89; operates in Mexico City, 91; opposition of sala del crimen to viceroy's appointment of successor to, 92
Velázquez, Miguel: activities as alcalde provincial of the hermandad, 32; as first judge of the acordada, 33; organizes procedures, 54–55; complaints of sala del crimen against, 71, 90
Vera Cruz, 57, 67, 80, 81, 83, 99, 103
Viceregal system: established under Antonio de Mendoza, 18; relations of with the audiencia, 22; inability of to maintain order, 27; establishment of acordada through, 33; deals with due process, 43; contains crime within acceptable limits, 51; helps support acordada financially, 56; cost to of acordada, 60; supervises expenses, 61; attitude of toward selection of judge, 64–65; and junta de revisión, 86; attitude of toward degree of order, 110
Vives, Juan Luis, 48

Xilotepec, 99
Xochimilco, 100

Yucatán, mescal legalized in, 103

www.ingramcontent.com/pod-product-compliance
Lightning Source LLC
Chambersburg PA
CBHW021712230426
43668CB00008B/812